THE ELEMENTS OF REINCARNATION

A T Mann was born in New York, graduated from Cornell University and worked as an architect in New York City and Rome before becoming a professional astrologer in 1972. He now lives and works in Copenhagen, Denmark as a teacher, author, architect, graphic designer and interactive multimedia designer.

The *Elements of* is a series designed to present high quality introductions to a broad range of essential subjects.

The books are commissioned specifically from experts in their fields. They provide readable and often unique views of the various topics covered, and are therefore of interest both to those who have some knowledge of the subject, as well as to those who are approaching it for the first time.

Many of these concise yet comprehensive books have practical suggestions and exercises which allow personal experience as well as theoretical understanding, and offer a valuable source of information on many important themes.

In the same series

The Aborigine Tradition
Alchemy
The Arthurian Tradition
Astrology
The Bahá'í Faith
Buddhism
Celtic Christianity
The Chakras
Christian Symbolism
Creation Myth
Dreamwork
The Druid Tradition
Earth Mysteries
The Egyptian Wisdom
Feng Shui
Gnosticism
The Goddess
The Grail Tradition
Graphology
Handreading
Herbalism
Hinduism

Human Potential
Islam
Judaism
Meditation
Mysticism
Native American
   Traditions
Natural Magic
Numerology
Pendulum Dowsing
Prophecy
Psychosynthesis
The Qabalah
The Runes
Shamanism
Sufism
Tai Chi
Taoism
The Tarot
Visualisation
Yoga
Zen

> **the elements of**

reincarnation
A T mann

ELEMENT

Shaftesbury, Dorset • Rockport, Massachusetts • Melbourne, Victoria

© Element Books Limited, 1995
Text © A T Mann 1995

First published in Great Britain in 1995 by
Element Books Limited
Shaftesbury, Dorset SP7 8BP

Published in the USA in 1995 by
Element Books, Inc.
PO Box 830, Rockport, MA 01966

Published in Australia in 1995 by
Element Books and
distributed by Penguin Books Australia Limited
487 Maroondah Highway, Ringwood,
Victoria 3134

Reissued 1997

Cover illustration by Max Fairbrother
Cover design by Max Fairbrother
Page design by Roger Lightfoot
Typeset by WestKey Ltd, Falmouth, Cornwall
Printed and bound in Great Britain by
Biddles Ltd, Guildford & King's Lynn

British Library Cataloguing in Publication
data available

Library of Congress Cataloging in Publication
data avialable

ISBN 1–86204–141–5

CONTENTS

As long as you do not contain
The truth of death and of rebirth,
An alien wanderer you remain
Upon a dark and troubled Earth.

Johann Wolfgang von Goethe

To my parents, who died young: Alden Taylor
Mann III (1918–1943) and Clara Gebhard Wakeley
(1920–1960)

Acknowledgements to John Baldock for his always
sensitive and perceptive editing of the text and his
helpful suggestions about content and illustrations.
To my wife Lise-Lotte for her support and
inspiration.

Introduction · What is Reincarnation?

One attaineth whatever state of being one thinketh about at the last when relinquishing the body, being ever absorbed in the thought thereof.

Sri Krishna to Arjuna, Bhagavad Gita, viii, 6

Reincarnation is the periodic reappearance of the soul in a succession of bodies. It is a doctrine which is central to many world religions such as Indian Vedanta, Pharaonic Egyptian, Greek and Roman polytheism, Buddhism, Taoism, Zoroastrianism, Sikhism, Gnosticism, shamanism, Sufism, Native American, African and many other faiths, and it is historically important in the development of Judaism, Christianity and Islam. Indeed, before the rise in influence of scientific materialism 200 years ago, reincarnation was a virtually universal belief of humanity.

Reincarnation and its mechanism of karma provide a natural morality and meaning for life, which lie beneath the surface of the major world religions and mystical philosophies – factors which are sadly absent in our present-day world.

The mechanism of reincarnation has always fascinated those who are reluctant to accept that this life is the beginning and end of existence. Have we lived before? Is there an afterlife?

1

Can this be all there is? We yearn for knowledge of the beyond–both of our past lives, where the influences which created us originated, and of our next lives, which will bring possibilities for greater understanding, resolution and fulfilment. Most importantly, we long to know how knowledge of past and future lives can enliven our current being here on earth.

But what is reincarnation and what are its laws? The law of karma is the universal process of cause and effect governing reincarnation and the transmigration of souls. According to the karmic view, the way we live now is the result of our actions in many past lives and in turn determines the quality of our future incarnations, in other bodies at other times. Psychic traces of our previous existences and their incomplete actions

Figure 1   The wheel of samsara

are passed on to us through our soul and manifest as the physical, mental, emotional and spiritual legacy we inherit at birth. The way we live this life is subsequently passed on through our soul to successive bodies when we die, in each life forming the essence of our new life's tasks. In accepting reality, we take responsibility not only for our own actions and their repercussions in this life, but also for resolving the burdens we have been accruing for many lives.

In Eastern religious philosophy, the endless cycles of birth, death and rebirth are symbolised by the wheel of samsara, liberation from which is enlightenment (*see* figure 1). The liberated soul resides in eternal bliss because, by not reincarnating (taking a body), it is free from desire and the endless wandering in the material world that this entails. This is in contrast to the bondage of modern Western culture, in which one is pressured to remain young and live for ever. The experience and understanding of the process of living in, rather than transcending, time is a primary difference between Western and Eastern religious traditions and philosophies.

These ideas are central to the modern ecological and spiritual paradigms now emerging in the world. If we do not reincarnate, why preserve the environment for the future? On the other hand, if we do, then it is imperative that we immediately modify our priorities of life. In investigating reincarnation, we will be able to understand more fully the implications of our own attitudes and beliefs about the world and our future in it.

Since the first humans wandered the face of the earth, we have attempted to comprehend and deal with the phenomenon of death and its relationship to the spirit. The oldest traces of human culture are men and women buried with their jewellery, tools and food in preparation for the afterlife. This seems primitive, but remember that we still bury the dead in elaborate coffins. Some people even explore the possibilities of cryogenic preservation of the body like the ancient Egyptians, or attempt to discover the secrets of eternal life through genetics. The mystery of life will always be with us.

Many influential authors, scientists, doctors, philosophers, psychologists, poets, politicians and others have believed in reincarnation. Their testimony is valuable because it has often been so subtly integrated into their works or ideas that it is obvious only when one looks deeply into their world views. Plato, Pythagoras, Ovid, Plotinus, Dante, Paracelsus, Kant, Goethe, Schopenhauer, Swedenborg, Blake, Schiller, Franklin, Emerson, Thoreau, Whitman, Nietzsche, Jung, to name but a few, have found the doctrine of reincarnation central to their philosophy.

A twelve-nation Gallup poll in 1969 found that between 18 and 25 per cent of Protestants and Catholics (religions which do not formally accept a belief in reincarnation) in the USA, Canada and major European countries such as the UK, Germany, Italy and France, accept the idea of rebirth[1]. Another poll on religion in 1981 revealed that 38 million Americans, almost one quarter of the population, admitted to being believers in reincarnation. It is clear, as our modern world view collapses, that reincarnation is fundamental in our search for meaning in the universe. It is a primary belief and one that is essential for us to understand.

In this book, I will be presenting what is known and surmised of the historical origins of reincarnation beliefs and bring these alive through the myths, stories, legends and epics which form the foundation of our collective world culture. Beyond history, our modern attitudes to this primal mystery will be explored, from regression therapy to the new and provocative search by physicists for the soul of the universe.

NOTES

[1] Gallup and Proctor, *Adventures in Immortality*, p.487.

1 · Discovering The Soul

The earliest humans wandered the earth and observed with awe and trepidation the movements of the sun, moon, planets and stars through the skies, the birth, transformation and death of the seasons throughout the year, and the birth and death of their own kind. In the thousands of millennia during which humans gradually became conscious, they mystically participated in the world around them. They lived with the animals in a Garden of Eden, but life was a fight for survival.

The mysteries of life and death pervaded their existence. They did not know from where they came nor how they got here, except from the womb of their mothers, and they could only worship the mysterious forces which apparently organised and ruled their world. Certainly the only possible meaning was survival. These early humans had no idea of evolution as we know it, only of survival. Although they were embedded within their world and of necessity attempting to be in tune with it, they also were different from the other animals with whom they shared the earth. They may even have felt like vulnerable intruders in a world populated by animals, their spiritual totems, and the gods and goddesses which governed natural processes like the sun, the moon, thunder, water, fire and earth. Similarly, they had little or no concept of individuality. Their social organization was tribal rather than familial, and there were few direct partnerships, only struggles to gain, retain and sustain dominance. The survival of the fittest prevailed and the strong dominated the sensitive.

Yet they knew that everyone eventually died and that their life left them in an instant. This was one of the first and most powerful mysteries in their essentially magical world, and the first artefacts of early humanity, dating back 50,000 or more years, show that they gave time, attention and great reverence to death. Some of the earliest traces of human culture are burials where the dead leaders were buried with sand, blossoms, weapons, clothing and ritual implements. The burial of the dead with ochre colouring for decoration and tools for killing food in the afterlife was one of the first ritual acts of a humanity separating itself from the animalistic and animistic world. This concern for the human spirit also points to their belief that they could survive to live again, either in a spirit world or again in the real world.

PRIMITIVE BELIEFS OF THE SOUL

Early humans came to believe that they possessed a soul which attended every moment of life, from birth to death. It was natural for them to liken this soul to breath, because when they died, they stopped breathing. In Latin the word for soul is *anima*, which means 'breath', as found in the word 'animate', 'to breathe life into'. The soul was seen as a double image of the person, a passive part which was split off from the living being at birth, but travelled with it through life, only to rejoin it in death. This double could be conceived as the divine part of the earthly being. When attempting to locate where the soul was during life, they imagined that it resided as an aura around the individual, as a shadow, or a reflection, or in body parts such as the penis, female reproductive organs, menstrual juices or seminal fluid.[1]

It was quite natural for them to attempt to explain what happened at death. It was obvious that the spark of life energy dissipated and disappeared at that moment. They therefore identified this mysterious something as the soul. In some

6

cultures it was taken to be a moth, a butterfly or some other such ethereal creature, which left the body and flew to the spirit world. In New Guinea it was thought that as death came near, the life essence or soul became very small in preparation for its departure. It had to leave the dying body somewhere, and what more natural place than through the mouth? The sound of the death-rattle confirmed this supposition.

SERPENTS SIGNALLING REBIRTH

Another common belief was that the soul escaped as a snake from the decaying body. The appearance of maggots after death could have had something to do with this belief, because it is a prevalent one, although the snake is also a symbol for the sexual *kundalini* life force which was also seen to survive the death of the body. In Australasia it is only the medicine man who turns into a snake at death, but in other cultures every death heralds the transformation into a snake or a worm.

Serpents of all types were identified with the magical soul, and therefore snakes, lizards and other reptiles were worshipped as gods of the dead, carrying great mystical power. The snake also carried sexual symbolism, as it was obviously shaped like and moved like a penis, and crawled into holes in the ground like the female sexual organs, or into deep waters. The serpent was therefore understood to be hermaphroditic, carrying qualities of both sexes.

For the African Meithei Raya, the serpent is both the external soul and the ancestor of the royal family, and serpents were always present at certain ceremonies in order to confer blessings upon their human descendants. Similarly, when the ritual serpent died it meant that the chief would die and that the tribe was in crisis; the fertility, libido or sexual energy of the tribe to procreate also seemingly died.[2]

Trees were also identified with processes of life and death. Mythically the tree was seen as the centre of the world because it had roots embedded deep in the earth but its branches spread into the sky. In this way it was a bridge which the soul traversed between what was above and what was below, or between the earthly and the heavenly worlds. It is easy to see how the tree and its life could be tied to the life of the soul.

According to the Tami of West Africa, the world banyan tree carried the soul-birds of the people. Every time a man was born a new leaf was created on the tree, and it remained there until he died, at which point it fell off. Each village was a branch, and its inhabitants were the leaves on that branch. Similarly, when a leaf was plucked from the tree, someone from that village would die. Sickness showed that the leaf was withering, and vice versa. The soul-birds were believed to pluck leaves from the world tree when it was time for individuals to die and go to the spirit world above.

European customs identify the soul with breath, clouds in the sky or birds in flight, and these identifications remain as folk traditions. The Scots believed that it was essential to leave windows open as death approached so that the soul could freely leave the body and escape to either the underworld or heaven. Tyrolean souls left by the mouth and became clouds in the sky, and in Hungary as doves flying away. Customs which existed throughout Europe well into the modern era included open windows, holes in the roof, or even the fumigation of the deathbed to create smoke in which the soul could escape.

The unconscious state of dreaming is believed to occur when the soul travels in search of new adventures or to complete the past. Thus when awakening, a Brazilian Indian believes that his soul has been away fishing or hunting during sleep, while his body has remained asleep in the hammock. The lack of differentiation between waking and sleeping imagery means that the gradation between consciousness and the unconscious is minimal.

When the soul is away during sleep, it is believed to be fatal to prevent it from returning. This is why in some tribes it is considered dangerous to wake someone while he or she is sleeping. Similarly the soul is also seen as inhabiting one's shadow, and if the shadow is stabbed, stepped upon or attacked in any way it will have a corresponding effect upon the soul. When someone's reflection is seen in water in some tribes, it is the soul which is seen, and this can be dangerous for that person, who will become sick or die because of it. Mirrors have the same mythology, because they are supposed to be able to capture the souls of living people in the house where someone has died. Photographs are also believed to capture the soul.

These customs show that the soul has throughout history been perceived as a powerful and important, if not *the* most important, part of a person and was treated with great respect. It was only natural that it was believed that at death the soul would be attracted to another body at some later time. It is this belief that is the foundation of reincarnation.

NOTES

[1] *Animism, Magic and the Divine King*, p 19.
[2] Ibid, p 17.

2 · MYSTERIES OF OSIRIS, ISIS, HORUS AND SET

When the sun god created the first divine being in Egypt, he spread his arms and endowed them with a *ka*, or soul. Indeed the hieroglyph of the *ka* is two extended arms at right angles to each other. To the Egyptians, the *ka* was the symbol of a person's existence. It was also the soul, as well as being a cipher of the individual. When Egyptians blessed someone's immortal *ka*, they were blessing that person. The *ka* was therefore treated as the protecting essence and vital force.[1] They imagined that every being contained a number of bodies, ranging in operation from the most spiritual to the most material. The *ka* was the stabilised animating spirit and is often represented by the symbol of the bull (or its horns), also because it is the principle of generation and manifestation (*see* figure 2).

There were two aspects of consciousness: the divine *ka*, which is a spiritual witness, and the intermediate *ka*, which is a permanent witness. In life the permanent witness integrates itself with animal consciousness, and upon death it unites with the spiritual witness and attains liberation.[2] Unless the permanent witness obeys the higher impulses of the spiritual witness,

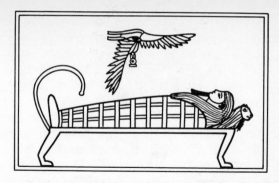

Figure 2 The soul – the ka – of a scribe visiting its mummified body

death may ensue and the spirit will be forced to be ruled in the other world by lower dispositions similar to those which it followed on earth.

To the Egyptians, the spiritual being wished for integration and liberation from successive births, deaths and rebirths, whereas the ego, with its insatiable appetite for the fruits of the world and the desires of the body, wished to remain in a body, and therefore competed with the *ka*s, whose power it envied. Images of Egyptian afterlife show the individual seeking his or her immortal *ka* in order to attain immortality.[3]

In the next life, the power of a strong ego will attract a new body and create a new life which amplifies its strength, but simultaneously moves it further from the guidance of its *ka*s. This may manifest in a life of physical control and the pursuit of power rather than one of spiritual accomplishment and sensitivity to the higher impulses. If this process continues, there is a danger that the spiritual witness will withdraw entirely, leaving the conscious 'I' to a dissolution called the second death, and condemning it to the animal, vegetable or mineral realm of its unfulfilled desires until it rises up through the chain of being to have another chance to be ensouled by spirit.

The Egyptians based their entire culture upon reincarnation and thereby produced a powerful and important religion. This in turn led to the creation of a profoundly mystical and symbolic architecture and art, which speaks to us through the ages of eternal gods weighing the soul after death against a feather. The beauty and power of their beliefs continue to fascinate and intrigue us.

However, this belief in reincarnation takes a unique form, expressed through the myth of the death and rebirth of the god Osiris, who became god of the dead. This mythology involved the quaternity of gods, Osiris, Isis, Horus and Set, and functioned at many levels (*see* figure 3). It was simultaneously a fertility myth associated with an agricultural society dependent upon the annual flooding of the River Nile, which provided fertile soil for the narrow band of farmlands along its banks; an astronomical myth which corresponded to the positions and movements of stars and planetary bodies, particularly the annual rising of the star Sirius, which signalled the flooding of the Nile; a political myth which represented the relationship between Upper and Lower Egypt, which were initially separate and then united into the singular Egyptian kingdom; and an exposition of profound spiritual principles

*Figure 3   The Egyptian gods Thoth, Isis, Nephys and Horus bless
a departing pharaoh in the process of becoming Osiris*

rooted in symbolism, central to which was the mummification and reincarnation of the god.

This central myth exists in many forms, no two of which are the same, yet their themes and symbolism are always identical. Some Egyptologists speculate that it was so familiar to the Egyptians (like the Old Testament to Jews and Christians) that there was never a reason to state it formally.[4] The general plot of the myth goes as follows:

> The celestial god Osiris was the son of the sky goddess Nut, and elder brother to Isis, Set, Nephthys and Anubis. He was the first king of Egypt and his consort was his sister Isis. Together with the god of writing, Thoth, Osiris gave the arts of civilization to humanity. Egypt prospered, but his brother Set was jealous. He murdered Osiris and cut his body into 14 pieces, which he scattered across Egypt, leaving no heir for the childless Isis. However, she collected the fragments and used her magical powers to recreate Osiris's body, thus making him the first mummy, and had sex with his dismembered phallus to become pregnant. Osiris was then metamorphosed into the constellation Orion and became ruler of the Kingdom of the Dead and overseer of the rituals of the dying. Isis hid in the marshes of the Nile and gave birth to a son, Horus, whom she raised to become a powerful prince. Upon becoming a man, Horus fought a duel with Set, during which he lost an eye and Set his testicles. The outcome of the battle was unclear, but ultimately Horus received the favour of the sun god and ruled Egypt as the first pharaoh and became the eternal eye of Ra.

The pharaonic cult involved a complex ritual where each pharaoh in turn was a reincarnation of Horus and his function was to uphold the law, symbolised by the goddess Maat. When a pharaoh died, he became one with Osiris in the underworld, while his successor became a new Horus-son and offspring of Osiris and Isis. The myth was therefore a dualistic one where the dying pharaoh was transformed from Horus into Osiris, while the newly crowned heir was simultaneously transformed into the Horus-son of Osiris waiting to become Osiris. It is easy to see how this was seen as a fertilization myth paralleling the birth, death and rebirth of the vegetation cycle of the natural world.

Symbolically Osiris is the fertilizing agent of the Nile, the earth is the body of Isis, and Horus is the moisturizing atmosphere. Set has a multiple symbolism, in that he is the enemy or antagonist of Osiris, Isis and Horus, the dividing principle of time and the intellect, and also the destroyer of life. In all myths we find the generative pair counterbalanced by the death principle. When the soul incarnates, death is the only possible end result of the process, followed by a rebirth. The myth is a symbolic enactment of the process of nature, the seasons and the natural functions which constitute them, and of the mystery of the death and resurrection of the natural world which was seen to be the prototype for the death and resurrection of the individual.

THE EGYPTIAN BOOK OF THE DEAD

The *Egyptian Book of the Dead* is one of the oldest books in the world. It is very complex, being composed of more than 100 papyrus chapters, and apparently came into being intact in a very short time, although its texts seem to have been carried by oral tradition before being written in beautiful illustrations and hieroglyphs in the Fifth Dynasty pyramids (*see* figure 4). Like most Egyptian religious texts, it was initially reserved for the kings, and is therefore directed at initiates or priests who were aware of the symbolic implications of their theology of rebirth. There are also many forms of the book, because later works were generally interpretations and glosses on the text of the original, but they all tell the same story.

It is a series of communications to the *ka* of the dead pharaoh, ensuring its identification with Osiris and encouraging it in its passage through the *duat* or underworld, through resurrection, in search of either liberation or rebirth. The message of the book is of one transformation: humans are not what they should and can be, they have a spark of divinity within them and it should be a foundation of their life work to translate that spark into a great illusion-consuming fire. The struggles of the pantheon of gods and goddesses can be seen on a symbolic level as the battles which take place within us all in the course of our lives, especially when we attempt to

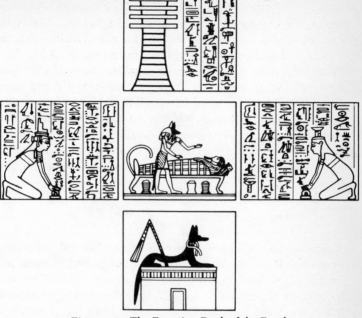

Figure   4   The Egyptian Book of the Dead

identify the soul within us and to direct our lives from that holy centre.

The texts are really guidebooks for the *ka*, and instruct the disembodied spirit in the procedures required to ensure eternal life. While the Egyptian underworld is not seen as a tangible place, it is the zone within which these transformations take place. The gods Ra and Osiris are polar opposites who rule the domains of the living and the dead respectively. Ra moves towards death during life, while Osiris, as the god of rebirth, moves towards life during death. Thus the dead king starts by being identified with Osiris, but as he accepts rebirth, he becomes Ra.

The territory in which this process happens is the celestial river, a metaphor for both the Nile and the Milky Way in the night sky, across which the barque of the gods sails. In this sense Ra is identified with the sun, which also dies each evening and descends under the earth as Osiris for its nightly passage through the underworld, only to be resurrected each morning anew. The goddesses of the 12 night-time hours (the *Houri*) accompany the god through his sojourn, and baboons symbolizing wisdom guide the *ka* through the underworld.

The dead king Osiris and the symbolic scarab are accompanied by a profusion of other sacred figures, including serpents representing the principle of time, gods wearing red and white headdresses representing Upper and Lower Egypt, and crocodiles waiting nearby to devour the soul in case it is found to be wanting in the process.

The entire process is a descent followed by an ascent, and each book recounts a stage through which the *ka* progresses as symbolised by its hour.[5] In each hour ritual certain initiations are intoned which identify the appropriate stage of the metamorphosis: a descent stage described above, and a larval stage signified by the presence of the scarab beetle Khephren, rolling its sphere of dung (a symbol of the sun), the nourishment of the larva, and the weaving of the cocoon, out of which its offspring magically appear and take flight towards the sun with their wings. The purely physical transformations of the life cycle of the scarab beetle serve as metaphors for the spiritual transformation of man: the dead Osiris who will rise as Horus.[6]

Throughout these stages, the departed is accompanied by elaborate scenes populated by the many animal gods and goddesses of Egyptian mythology. The water snake shows the immersion in the underworld of the unconscious animalistic world of the dead: the flesh-eating jackal or dog Anubis is the opener of the way, and his presence shows that the body is consumed in the mystery of death and rebirth. The egg stage brings the appearance of the goddess Isis as a weaver, who supervises the creation of the cocoon and who also leads the solar barque heavenwards across the sky. Similarly the god Thoth with his baboon counterparts lead the barque into the transformation process. Intertwined serpents suggest lunar cycles, which may be a way of saying that the rebirth process takes a number of lunar cycles, or that the time of rebirth will be timed by the moon's cycles.

EGYPTIAN SYMBOLS OF REBIRTH

Towards the end of the ritual process, symbols of rebirth begin to occur, particularly the ankhs and palm branches possessed by gods who create trees and greenery. In the final moments the god Horus oversees the last phases of the process. From the primal waters come snakes which become the spinal column, with the scarab as the head. Eventually the whole body is brought together and the now disused mummy of the dead king is discarded to the darkness, while Horus joins the newly created body in his new home of flesh.

Images of the process described in the *Egyptian Book of the Dead* are often referred to as the Last Judgement because among the assembly of all the gods and goddesses in the hall of judgement, the heart of the dead is weighed by Anubis against a feather, his *Maat* or the sum of the possibilities of his life. The values and qualities made manifest in the life are shown in a life record kept by the god-scribe Thoth. If the life was sincere the soul passes on, but if not the heart is fed to the devouring animals of conscience. The soul of the deceased is shown by the hawk wings which adorn his head. After the judgement scene, the unformed body of the next life lies awaiting the impression of the soul and the new tasks which it will inherit. Osiris waits as Horus leads the *ka*, now trans-figured and radiant as a solar disk, into the light and into the presence of the Inner Circle of Humanity.[7]

The psychological symbolism of the Egyptian rituals are profound, particularly as they seem to have been the basis for subsequent Hindu, Buddhist and even Christian judgements. The events of our lives are evaluated following the moment of death, and this judgement is the foundation of the next life we will take. It is profoundly powerful that not only are the traces of our last life brought into this life, but the issues we face in this life are also transmitted into the next. This mythology brings the cosmic process of reincarnation into a great and rich perspective.

NOTES

1. *Animism, Magic and the Divine King*, p 17–18, where the author presents the Roman concept of the genius as being the serpent energy, the strength and the procreative power of an individual.
2. Schwaller de Lubicz, *The Opening of the Way*, p 150.
3. Ibid, p 150–4.
4. Bauval & Gilbert, *The Orion Mystery*, p 92.
5. West, *The Traveler's Key to Ancient Egypt*, pp 281–313, describes the funerary texts in the Cairo Museum in a profound and clear way.
6. Ibid, p 293.
7. Collin, *The Theory of Eternal Life*, Plate IV caption.

3 · DREAMS OF MAYA AND THE WHEEL OF SAMSARA

As a man casts off his worn-out clothes and takes on other new ones, so does the embodied soul cast off its worn-out bodies and enters other new ones.

Bhagavad Gita, ii, 22

Reincarnation is a fundamental principle of Hindu religion and its Vedantic school of philosophy. Individual souls reincarnate through vast world ages called *yugas*, everything is created, and then destroyed, and then recreated again. The idea that life is a cyclical process permeates their world view at all levels, from the shortest spans of time to the longest.

According to the Hindu creation epics, the creator and sustaining god Vishnu participates in a continual and repeating cosmic myth which requires that after his own death he will take a new body, reincarnate and again bring the world into manifestation. As soon as he does so, powerful egotistical, demonic forces also instantly manifest, their sole function being to oppose him. They do everything they can to dominate him, destroy him or subvert his creation. Although this seems a negative process, on the contrary, the battle between opposing forces is seen as being the essential nature of the world, and resistance is the dynamic force which sustains the world.

Brahman symbolises undifferentiated consciousness, which is composed of the trinity of being-consciousness-bliss. Behind outer appearances, which are symbolised by the goddess Maya as the creative vehicle of Brahman, is the independent, imperishable universal Self, called *ātman*. Therefore Brahman/*ātman* are the components of universal consciousness which are made manifest by Maya.

THE ETERNAL *ĀTMAN*

The primary objective of Hindu philosophy and religion is to penetrate the mysteries of being and restore unity with the eternal spiritual world of *ātman*, which is outside of time, lying behind appearances. *Jivatman* is the individual, finite consciousness apparently possessed by the infinity of beings which compose the world, but which, through the cosmic illusion, appear to be separate from *ātman*/Brahman. *Jivatman* is the equivalent of what we call the soul.

Thus the soul originates in Brahman or *ātman*, but is split off from the primordial unity, separated from it by the guile and illusions of Maya. Everything in the physical world is in perpetual change, but *ātman* never changes because it is beyond space and time, and therefore impervious to causality. The goal of enlightenment (*moksha*) is to eliminate the ignorance (*avidya*) which separates *jivatman* from *ātman*, that is, to make knowledge of the Self the universal factor in being. On an individual level the task is to transmute the heart from a state of bondage to the physical world and its enticements, past human imperfection and ignorance, to its ultimate function as an organ of transcendent earthly existence.[1]

The soul is eternal but carries the *jiva*, or illusion that it is separate from *ātman*. As such it has always existed and will always exist, unless it attains enlightenment and escapes from the round of birth and rebirth. There are seen to be an infinity of souls which have always existed back through time and which, although being neither male nor female, take on male and female bodies. Every individual ego is a psycho-physical entity containing a soul which is typically unaware of its eternal past and linkage with all other souls. The ego is therefore a temporary expression of the *ātman* or eternal soul which is understood to be enclosed within a series of layers, sheaths or bodies which it discards at death, only to reincarnate into another set of bodies in a new incarnation.

There are three bodies: the gross physical body of the organism, the invisible subtle body (called the *linga sharira*) and the causal body. At the death of the gross body the subtle body survives to pass on modifications or traces (*samskaras*) of the past life to a new gross vehicle in an incoming incarnation. The subtle body is termed the mind (which is different from our Western concept of mind as relating to the brain), and is composed of a series of 17 traits and perceptions, which it carries throughout a human life and on to other lives, although it also contains what we would consider the emotions. It is the accumulation of *samskaras* which reincarnate through the subtle body, attract a developing embryo in the womb of a mother, and simultaneously integrate with and transform the genetic characteristics of that potential being according to its karma.[2] Souls incarnate in a succession of bodies in an attempt to achieve liberation, which is identification with the eternal. This entire process is automatic in that it does not require consciousness to motivate it, but it constitutes the foundation of cosmic law.

REDEMPTION FROM KAMA

The mythology and doctrines of Hinduism both express the concept that the world arises from individual *ātman* seeking redemption. Kama (*see* figure 5) is the Hindu god of love, and like the Greek Eros was the first-born of the gods after Chaos. He governs the realm of desires (*Kama-loka*) and embodies the principle of fulfilment, but he carries the most powerful curse as well. Those who forget the Self remain attached to his realm, and are doomed to eternal travel around the wheel of *samsara* (*see* figure 1) the round of time which leads from sex to conception to birth to old age and, inevitably, death. The

Figure 5 The Hindu god of love Kama and his consort

character of our unfulfilled thoughts and desires, which are under the guidance of Kama, is what impels us to reincarnate back into the world again and again. The fruit of this desire is our destiny.

The Hindu universe is divided into many parts, but the most basic division is into three realms: infernal, earthly and celestial. The eternal Self can change from one to the other and back again, according to the quality and nature of our thoughts and desires. The lower, infernal realms signify the total dominion of desires, and these hells are animalistic, and inhabited by giant monsters, terrifying beasts and the even more horrific spectres which are, however, merely ghosts of the imagination.

Also in this realm are the gods and goddesses of earlier cults such as Titans, goblins, naga water-gods and the whole pantheon of household deities. In the middle, earthly realm, signifying those beings which are in the thrall of desire but still have opportunities to free themselves from it, are humans and beasts on the earthly plane, ruled by Kama. Above this world is a celestial world of those who are beyond the fundamental bondage of desire, which is also ruled by Kama in his higher being, and which is inhabited by winged birdlike gods and goddesses (the *garudas*) and the celestial musicians, who are humans reborn into realms of pleasure and sexuality. Above them still are the higher deities, until one approaches the realm of the formless and purely spiritual beings which exist above and beyond manifestation in eternal bliss. Kama in his divine will to procreate is responsible for the round of incarnation in these realms, but this is also the reason why the universe continues to exist, so that all beings can potentially inhabit this highest plane of existence.

At death we travel through all these domains, from the pure formless spiritual one down through the various paradises and hells, until we become attracted to the domain which is compatible with working through the unfulfilled desires which we have brought with us from our last life. Progress through the states is slow and arduous because beings tend to want to remain the same, to attempt to satisfy the same unfulfillable desires and, whether successful or not, to continue to pursue them. If one is obsessed by sexuality, no sexual experiences are ever enough to satisfy the basic desire which lies behind the fantasy or illusion of sexuality, and therefore one is well ensnared in the web of Maya.

In India there is a powerful identification with social roles, and this rigidity corresponds to this image of continual rebirth without end, recircling the *samsara* wheel endlessly, with little possibility for movement, either up or down. Indeed the kinds of identification with and classification of things in the world which are so prized by the Western mind constitute the primary instruments of bondage to the Eastern spirit. The outer qualities which differentiate things from one another are precisely the tools and constituents of the world of Maya. As long as one makes choices, expresses ideas or desires, or makes an effort to be something in the world, one is ensuring continued and deepening bondage to the world.

The only antidote to the web of Maya is the release of distinctions, which leads to an identification with everything in the world, with the whole of the creation, or in other words, being at one with Brahman. As divinity resides in all things, it does not matter at the most fundamental level which aspect of divinity one worships. Therein lies the great dilemma of Hindu religion, and the primary justification for a caste system of social bondage which echoes and reflects the spiritual bondage of Indian views of religion, karma and reincarnation. The only path to freedom is the elimination of any thoughts of the gods, the pathways or ideals of the *dharma* (path of virtue). The most valued quality is that of being continually alive in enlightenment.

The revered saints of Hinduism are traced through many lifetimes, a succession of divine birthrights, sometimes even through animal planes of existence, where they demonstrate that even in such form their higher qualities are evident and transform all beings around them. In many cases these reincarnation genealogies are creatively adjusted so that the spirituality embodied by the saint has a manifestation on every possible level.

Some believe that not all souls reincarnate at the same rate. More evolved beings have the capability to reincarnate more frequently to learn further lessons and to act as disseminators of the process, while the masses tend to reincarnate less frequently, if at all. They are ignorant of their own possibilities, and are quite happy to remain so. This system creates spiritual goals towards which the lay person can aspire, and ultimately results in the concept of many spheres or heavens, each of which has its own complex hierarchy, rulers and qualities. For higher beings, the interludes between lives are often blissful and beautiful, almost a kind of cosmic holiday while resting before the next challenge of rebirth.

The earliest Vedic gods had human and animal forms, although no human could ever hope to reach their exalted plane, but Dravidian Indians did accept that even the highest gods and goddesses were simply individual souls who had merited bliss.[3] When their merit expired they often vacated their places in favour of others, and descended again into human, animal or demonic form. This continual transformation seemed to reflect the workings of the world around them, and certainly made for a colourful and extremely dramatic spiritual mythology.

JAINISM AND THE REALMS OF THE GODS

Jainism is an offshoot of the Hindu religion which theoretically originated in prehistoric times, but was in reality started by the Jains' primary saint, whom they see as the last of the line of their *tirthankaras*, Vardhamana Mahavira. He was a contemporary of the Buddha and died in the 6th century BCE.[4] The supreme godhead *tirthankara* gods are the objects of contemplation and the goals of human activity. In the world of reincarnating souls taking new bodies with every new life, these creating, preserving and destroying gods exist in a sphere separate from all the others.

The Jains represent their living organism of a universe as two identical rings around an archetypal domain in the middle of the world separated by a river, across which only the *tirthankaras* may pass. The gods thus live in a higher, more central, pure and exalted realm which is only available to the lay person after a multitude of lifetimes passing through the less exalted domains.

To the Jains, every being is a monad, a single imperishable unit of life, which ascends and descends through the chain of being from humanity down to the demonic and animal states, as well as up to the ultimate heavens, through endless transformations. The higher the aspiration and evolution of a monad, the more qualities and faculties it carries with it. It incarnates into bodies and yet remains a subtle substance beyond the body. It is seen as permeating the body and emitting a glowing aura, a subtle halo of light which is perceptible to clairvoyant or enlightened sight. A monad contains particles of karma, like an iron which is made red with intense heat, which communicates life tasks to the body which it animates.

The level of evolution of a life-monad can be seen in the karmic taste, fragrance and quality of which it is composed, but all are expressed through its colour. There are six colours, each of which signifies a specific state of purity and karmic level of being. The two lowest colours are *tamas* or dark; the middle two are *rajas* or fiery (3 is smoky grey and 4 is flame red); and the higher two are luminous and clear and signify the *sattvas* of virtue, goodness and clarity. Jain colour symbolism reflects this hierarchy: black is for cruel or raw people; dark blue is for rogues or the venal; grey is for thoughtless or uncontrolled people; red is for magnanimous, honest and devout people; yellow shows compassionate, considerate and controlled people; and the highest white souls are impartial and dispassionate.[5] It is obvious that the desirable evolution is towards increased clarity and light, and one can see in people the extent to which they have achieved this in their being. Virtuous acts increase the clearness of the monad, while evil acts darken it. But even the good acts link the life-monad to the world, albeit through gentler ties.

The ultimate goal for the Jain is to be released and to attain *nirvana* by abstaining from all action in the world and living a life of contemplation, which is a rejection of life itself. To the Jain saints reality was merely a shell to be pierced and dissolved. However, as negative as this seems, by reaching this plateau one becomes a 'crossing-maker', passing over into the super-divine world of bliss and endless pleasure, beyond even the gods and goddesses and their powers. Paradoxically, by a total negation of the world, one attains all worldly pleasures beyond the world. This implies that by the act of their attainment, such pleasures become valueless. The ultimate Jain saint Parsvanatha attained this state, achieved perfect enlightenment, but renewed it by returning and teaching the timeless doctrine.

Beliefs such as those of the Jain that are often inconceivable to Westerners bent upon living as fully and as long as possible in the world (of desire). The concept of the personality and the body as meaningless masks veiling the essence of a divine world is in many ways the opposite of the principles practised in our modern world. We can learn much from their beliefs.

26

NOTES

[1] Zimmer, *Philosophies of India*, p 4.
[2] Hick, *Death and Eternal Life*, pp 312–17.
[3] Ibid, p 184.
[4] Ibid, p 182.
[5] Ibid, p 230.

4 · BUDDHIST NO-SOUL AND REBIRTH

I remembered many, many former existences I had passed through: one, two births, three, fifty . . . a hundred thousand, in various world-periods.

Gautama Buddha, adapted by Sogyal Rinpoche in
The Tibetan Book of Living and Dying

Buddhism is based upon the teachings of Gautama the Buddha (563–483 BCE), but the word 'buddha' means 'one who is enlightened to the meaning of life', therefore Buddhist philosophy is the accumulation of thousands of years of spiritual teachings and many thousands of buddhas.

Reincarnation is a central concept of Buddhism because the Buddha achieved enlightenment as a result of many lifetimes of sustained work, although here a contradiction arises. The primary difference between Buddhist and Hindu or Jain doctrines of reincarnation has to do with the definition of exactly what it is that incarnates. In Hinduism it is the immortal soul, *ātman*, which takes up successive bodies in order to work out its karma. In Buddhism the soul itself is seen as an ephemeral illusion. The Buddha, while not specifically denying its existence, nevertheless did not refer to *ātman* as the vehicle or cause of the suffering he perceived as the condition

28

of life. Many of his later followers developed the idea of the not-self as a primary doctrine. As a result, Buddhists refer to the process as rebirth rather than as reincarnation, which assumes the existence of a soul. The Buddhist term *anatta* means soullessness (no-*ātman*) and implies a rejection of the Hindu concept of the universal Self as the central mechanism of being. The continuum in Buddhism is the eternal quality of mind or consciousness, which are interchangeable terms. This subtle mind continues to exist, changing form and level, but remaining in existence for all eternity.

The Buddha himself was more concerned with moral and ethical values than with metaphysical speculation about the vehicles or mechanics of incarnation. A foundation of his teachings is the Sanskrit phrase '*sat om tat*', which can be freely translated as 'this is that'. The primary concern in life should be the journey itself rather than that which makes the journey. But if there is nothing to reincarnate, what is it that is reborn, and how can reincarnation be central to Buddhism?

An act of will is a creative force which inevitably leads to effects in the physical world, ie, incarnation. The thought-force of a sentient being, generated by the will to live and the desire to enjoy sensory experiences, produces after death another being which is the causal result of the preceding one.[1] This Theravada Buddhist explanation of incarnation does not define soul, but implies that it is the expressed thought-form (a manifestation of mind) which moulds the energetic coming-into-being of an embryo as a causal force leading to incarnation. As to what it is that incarnates, it is the wilful energies, not the specific vehicle which expresses them. Buddhists have often identified other concepts like 'character' or 'I' which reincarnate, but such explanations are just gestures to the common people rather than core Buddhist doctrine. Because it is these wilful energies that incarnate, the essential teaching in Buddhism is to still the will and eliminate as much as possible any desires which could lead to further incarnations. Rather than use the term 'reincarnation', however, Buddhists call the process 'transmigration'.

When the Buddha meditated under the bodhi tree in his quest to attain enlightenment, he broke through all forms of being and entered the timeless void, in which the Hindu god Kama appeared to him as a youth carrying a flute and tried to tempt him from his task. Kama embodies the wonderful pleasures of existence as motivated by the principle of love, but he is also the god of death because by enticing the spirit into manifestation (life) he eventually requires the ultimate price to be paid, which is death and rebirth.[2] The great paradox of which the Buddha became aware is that the more overwhelming the potential blissful pleasures of the world, the more excruciating is the knowledge that one cannot escape from the bounds of the world in even thousands of incarnations.

THE TIBETAN BOOK OF THE DEAD

According to both Hinduism and Buddhism the last thought at the moment of death determines the character of the next incarnation.[3] For this reason these thoughts must be rightly directed, either psychically by the dying person if she or he has been initiated, or by a lama, guru or friend, if not. According to Tibetan Buddhism, after death the soul detaches from the physical body and undergoes a profound and powerful purification ritual. It passes through the *bardo* states, stages through which the soul's status and progress is tested against past karma as a preliminary to choosing a new womb for reincarnation. The descriptions of the bardo states have been analysed extensively by the Tibetan Buddhists and form the foundation of their famous *Tibetan Book of the Dead*. They have also been investigated by many modern psychotherapists, because in addition to providing guidance for the soul after death, they symbolize important psychic processes for the living.[4]

The Tibetan Book of the Dead (Sanskrit: *Bardo Thîdol*) is a book of instructions for the dead and dying, as well as for the living. The bardo is a period of 49 days between death and rebirth, and is divided into three prominent stages. The first describes what occurs psychically at the moment of death, the second deals with the dream-state which intervenes in the time after death, and the third is the appearance of birth instincts which lead inexorably to prenatal events and birth.

The passage through the bardo states begins with an

entrance into a white light of unimaginable power and purity, a merging with the godhead. Immediately after the death of the physical body, the principle of consciousness is shown glimpses of nirvana, supreme insight and illumination, and at this point it has its greatest opportunity to achieve liberation from the cycle of rebirths. But the soul has typically become so strongly identified with and attached to a body with its feelings and ideas, as well as to physical objects, possessions, sensations or spiritual drives acquired during the incarnation, that it cannot detach itself cleanly. Unless these cravings are eliminated, the soul yearns to return to the physical plane, and is reborn in another body. These attachments or appetites force it to incarnate back onto the wheel of existence, which the Buddhists consider the domain of sorrow and death. Once this initial opportunity just after the death process has passed, the soul descends into more illusory realms which are successively more terrifying and entrapping, and during which it is extremely important that someone guide it towards its next incarnation, and explain the nature of the visions which happen spontaneously.

The descent through the bardo states is portrayed as a descent into hell, in which vast times pass in extremes of heat and cold. The principle of consciousness is devoured by wild beasts or incinerated by fires, only to reappear instantly, and generally undergoes extremely arduous trials and tribulations. These trials are metaphors for the decay and purification of the deceased physical body and the creation of a new body from raw material carrying deep desires. The culmination of the bardo process is the discovery of a new womb and rebirth into the world. In many ways the experiences of the bardo states are like being consumed by one's desires, or alternatively, like returning to human life by repeating all the earlier stages of planetary and earthly evolution in a highly condensed way. In some senses it is like a virtual experience of reality, as a teaching device.

Buddhist beliefs directly contradict those of the modern West, where most people would like to live for ever, whatever the form of their suffering. Buddhists consider the physical plane a suffocating captivity in relation to the higher, more spiritual dimensions, which are liberating. Their object in incarnating is to become free of desire and thus to be liberated from the need to reincarnate. The supreme paradox is that the primary Buddhist teaching, which is repeated during the death ritual, is an initiation into the domain of life, just as during life the teachings are preparations for death. In this sense, the Buddhist teachings are like the secret religious teachings of other cultures, particularly the Egyptian and Greek mysteries (*see* Chapters 2 and 5).

Experiences similar to, if not identical with, the bardo states have been described by those who have had near-death experiences (sometimes abbreviated as NDEs). Most talk about a heavenly white light, the rising of the soul from the dying body, and an ascent into higher realms.

During the between-life states the soul goes all the way back to creation and recapitulates the entire process over again, in a concentrated period, in preparation for emerging from the womb at birth. After birth, the newly incarnate soul gradually forgets the experiences and lessons of previous lives and of the bardo states. Usually it is only very early in childhood or at the approach of death that memories of previous states return, unless exceptional experiences in life activate them.

Successive cycles of birth, death and rebirth are symbolised by the *wheel of samsara*, as the soul experiences many levels of being, searching for completion and balance. Some suggest that the purpose of the initiation process is to restore the soul to the state of divinity it lost at birth.[5] Liberation from the process, which is freedom from the need to live yet more lives, is enlightenment. Those who experience NDEs often find that their lives and their perspectives on life are profoundly changed, and become more spiritual. This is how the bardo states affect the soul. These effects are similar to that of the bodhisattvas, those beings who, through compassion for all sentient beings, postpone their own enlightenment so that they can work for the enlightenment of others.

In his commentary for the Evans-Wentz translation of *The Tibetan Book of the Dead*, Carl Jung suggested that in psychoanalytic circles the experiences of the bardo states were seen to parallel the exploration of the psychic content of intrauterine gestation and early childhood in Freudian psychoanalysis. As Freud was initially concerned with sexual fantasies, this is appropriate, because if the soul resists the first teachings of the bardo states, it will be subject to all kinds of bizarre sexual scenes, visions of mating couples, and these will lead it towards rebirth. The more it is embedded in the instinctive sphere in life, the greater the chance that it will be drawn towards the lower bardo states, and subsequently attract a new incarnation which reflects its entrapment in desire. Jung believed that this was characteristic of some practitioners of Western psychology and of the Western psyche in negatively valuing the unconscious and considering it entirely personal, rather than both personal and universal. As a result, he suggested that the best way for a Westerner to read the book was backwards, ie from rebirth back towards the point of death.

The process by which an incarnating soul selects a new body is complex. The developing embryo carries a genetic heritage which the soul must use as raw material for expressing its next stage of development. The more specific the karmic traces or vestiges of unresolved issues from past lives, the more direct the attachment with the next life and the next body, and the more difficult it is to achieve liberation. Indeed, one way to define karma for the Western mind is to consider it to be our 'psychic heredity', composed of those inherited characteristics which express themselves psychologically. Jung also suggested that we inherit *archetypes* (ideological constituents) of the collective unconscious, the term he formulated to describe the universal dispositions of the mind which are not confined to race or family lineage and which constitute a deeper layer of the human psyche. Within this context, the Tibetan knowledge is a schema which echoes both Western psychotherapy and also the inner, subtle workings of genetics.

WORLD AGES

The Buddhist world view is cyclical and reflects on the macro scale the same dynamics as exist in the micro scale in individual reincarnation. History has many cyclical time periods, from blinks of ⅕ second to *yugas* (ages of humanity) of tens of thousands of years, to *mahayugas* (great ages of the universe) of hundreds of millions of years. Each world age is structured like a lifetime, beginning with a conception and a birth and ending with a death. Successive world ages diminish in length, reflecting a deterioration of the quality of life. In the original Golden Age humans lived for thousands of years, while in the Kali Yuga, the present and last age, lifetimes are shorter and more decadent, and illness is endemic. At the end of the Kali Yuga the universe will dissolve in a great conflagration, the *praylaya*, at which point the entire process will start over again.

One implication of such vast cyclical world ages is that a single human lifetime seems insignificant by comparison. The desire to live for ever directly contradicts the ideal of a Buddhist or Hindu, who wishes to be liberated from the need to incarnate again, to be free from the misery of existence, and to escape from the wheel of karma. In Eastern religions, the pain and bondage of life on the physical plane is only compensated for by the prospect of freedom from it. Their life philosophy is an inversion of ours. They devalue the material in favour of the spiritual, which has profound effects upon their attitude to life. This is why it is important that we understand and acknowledge both Eastern and Western philosophies and psychologies.

NOTES

[1] Head and Cranston, *Reincarnation*, p 64.

[2] Indeed, as we saw in Chapter 3, the state of purgatory in which the recently deceased soul chooses its next womb for rebirth is called the *Kama-loka* (the domain of Kama), and the choice is based primarily upon unfulfilled desires carried over from previous lives.

[3] Evans-Wentz, *The Tibetan Book of the Dead*, from the commentary by C G Jung, p xviii.

[4] See especially Sogyal Rinpoche, *The Tibetan Book of Living and Dying*.

[5] Evans-Wentz, *The Tibetan Book of the Dead*, from the commentary by C G Jung, p xii.

5 · GREEK MYSTERIES

To him who, purified, would break this vicious round
And breathe once more the air of heaven – greeting!
Orphic Golden Tablet

Ancient Greek philosophy was integral to its religion. It is generally recognised that Orpheus was the founder of Greek theology, science and art, and originator of the first mystery cults in Greece, which in turn provided the inspiration from which the Greek belief in reincarnation arose. While there are doubts about his actual existence, he symbolized the mystery religion of the Greeks, which was almost certainly derived from those of the Egyptians and Hindus. G. R. S. Mead suggests that the Egyptian, Chaldean, Bacchic, Orphic, Eleusinian and other mystery cults all came from a common source.[1] This may be a natural and obvious result of the fact that the Indo-Aryan people who settled Greece originally came from the East and were then diffused throughout Europe.

Orpheus was identified by the Renaissance Hermetic Marsilio Ficino as being in the line of succession of the chief magus Zoroaster and the Egyptian god Hermes Trismegistus, and his teachings were passed on through Pythagoras and Plato. The myth recounts that Orpheus was the first poet and an inspired singer, the fruit of a liaison between one of the Muses and a King of Thrace. Apollo taught him to play the seven-stringed lyre so divinely that people, animals, stones and even the gods and goddesses worshipped at his feet. But tragedy was in store for this divine mortal. While fleeing a wicked seducer, his dear wife Eurydice was bitten by a serpent, died and went to Hades. In the madness of grief he charmed the god of the underworld with his playing so that Eurydice was allowed to return to earth again, on condition that Orpheus did not look back as they left. As they recrossed the boundary, he could not help himself. At the last step, doubting whether she was really following him, he turned, and Eurydice was instantly taken away from him. He then either died of grief, or was killed by Zeus's lightning for revealing the sacred mysteries to mortals.

The Orphic mystery religion was transmitted by sacred hymns, and taught that the soul was immortal and the body merely a prison in which it was trapped from birth to death. Upon death the soul experienced the mysteries of the in-between world for a short time, only to be reborn in another body, and so on, *ad infinitum*. It entered a body, committed sins, expiated them, underwent punishment in the invisible world, and then passed to a new body. The soul in an Orphic sense is similar to the Hindu *ātman* or *purusha*, both meaning aspects of the universal Self. There was also an Orphic equivalent of the *samsara* round, which they called the cycle of generation, although Orpheus simply called it 'the wheel'.

THE ORPHIC LYRE

The Orphic cosmology was similar to the Hindu in having a system of historical cycles with alternating manifestations and reabsorptions of the universe from the primordial void, which was called the Orphic egg or the cosmic egg. This was the origin of Plato's later theory of world ages. There had been earlier races of humanity which perished in a flood, and these correspond to the Atlanteans described by Plato in the *Timaeus*. It was also believed that after the seventh world age there would follow the destruction and then the salvation of a divine race at the end of time.

According to the Orphic mystery rites the soul is a monad (a unity), but has three vehicles in incarnation: an ethereal, an aerial and a terrestrial. The ethereal corresponds to the luminous soul which lives in bliss in the stars. The aerial is a kind of repository for memories of previous existences which suffers punishment for sins after death and before rebirth. The terrestrial is the inhabitant of earth, the physical body. Since Plato was initiated into the Orphic mysteries, his description of the relationship between these aspects of the soul are in essence Orphic. The ethereal is non-material, the aerial is part spiritual and part material, and the terrestrial body is all material, but is a composite of all three.

The relationship between the three bodies was expressed in various mathematical proportions and harmonic ratios which corresponded to the seven strings of Orpheus's lyre. Indeed this was the source of the Platonic and Pythagorean magical numerology and its function was to relate the world soul to the individual soul through these mystical numbers and their sequence. The numbers which became the magical instrument called the Lyre of Apollo demonstrated the evolution of nature in the universe and the key to balancing the spheres and to integrating the power of planetary movements into the wisdom of the soul. Because a human was a mirror of the universe, his or her nature could be tuned to the divine nature using these techniques, and become a master of cosmic powers. But in order to do this it was necessary to live a life according to Orphic purification rituals and discipline, both physically and psychologically.

PYTHAGORAS – HE WHO REMEMBERS HIS INCARNATIONS

Pythagoras was a Greek philosopher who founded a mystery school based on principles he learned during his sojourn in Egypt and supplemented it with an Orphic initiation. Indeed his very name meant 'he who remembers his incarnations'. The foundation of his reincarnation belief was the process of trans-migration, in which the spirit wanders through lives, occupy-ing bodies as it pleases: now a beast, now a human, and back again, but never perishing.

The key to evolving through the spheres towards the divine depended upon following a morality which also came from above. This required: constant and regular prayer in which one asked for nothing; sacred filial duty to parents; the exercise of gratitude towards others; observance of chastity before marriage; marriage as a spiritual tie rather than an animal sexual union; greater love for one's partner than for oneself; and the initiation of children into the mysteries. Indeed, like the Indian sacerdotal system, it was recommended that those who wished to join the priesthood should first marry and have children before they withdrew from the world. This similarity supports the belief that Pythagoras travelled to India during his long life.

The most profound beliefs of Pythagoras concern instructions for the process of death and rebirth. The Pythagoreans believed that a primary function of life was *mathesis*, which is to remember the previous knowledge of the soul. Such reminiscence is an eternal productive principle in soul life, the inner nature of things, and the essence of cosmology and of the mysteries concerning death.

At death the aerial body, which is a spirit body composed of various proportions of the four elements: earth, water, air and fire, leaves the physical body and passes into the invisible world (which corresponds to the Hindu *Kama-loka*), where it pays its penalties for the evils of its past life, in addition to receiving care for its transformation of sensation, purified by pain. If the soul were without a body it would not feel any of this, so the spirit body, rooted in the physical world, is what experiences pain and redemption. If the soul was able to detach itself from this aerial body, it would ascend to the heavens and not incarnate again.

Pythagoras believed that even diet affected the purity of the aerial body, and hence one's ability to transcend the round of incarnations. A pure and carefully chosen diet makes the body less susceptible to the gross energies to which it is exposed in this and other worlds. For this reason, part of the Orphic mysteries involved ritual purification through washing and fasting, as well as the use of purgatives.

Although it seems strange that the invisible body should have the sensitivity to diet of the more tangible body, this is because it does control the lower body. The analogy given by

Aristotle is that of a crystal which takes on the colouring of anything around it, and light passing around or through it. Being numinous, the spirit body can be transformed into almost any shape and colour, and is therefore extremely sensitive.

Over many incarnations the soul stays in physical bodies until it has purified itself sufficiently to be freed from the round of generations. The implication is that pure body leads to pure soul. The passionate nature of the desire function, which influences the aerial body, can be laid aside only when the life itself also reflects these higher concerns.

The radiant causal body was eternally united with the soul and sensitive to the influences of the stars, primarily because it was starry in itself. As the soul was cosmic, it was this quality or aspect of it which responded to the energies in the cosmos and which was the agent of astrological influences. The ethereal body was the chariot of the soul. It may be that this quality informed the tarot major arcana card the Chariot (*see* figure 6), because it never stopped moving and contained all the senses. This subtle vehicle of the soul was what enlightened beings possessed if they had worked out their destiny and become one with it.

The essential teaching of the Orphic mysteries was to die continually in life, which meant to forgo desires and passions in preparation for the final judgement, and to subjugate the desire functions of all the bodies in preparation for losing them after death. Whichever virtues a person chose to identify with during life determined which level of body they would be governed by after death. Practical awareness was of the gross physical body; purifications were of the subtle body; intellect and spirituality were of the causal body; and contemplation of the supreme union with God. The perfect human has a rational soul with an envelope of purified bodies, while angels are souls with only aerial bodies.

The specific reincarnation beliefs of the Orphics were the foundation of those of Pythagoras and Plato and their schools. The fundamental belief was that the soul is imprisoned in the body, which was sometimes referred to as the sepulchre or tomb. They even spoke about those souls imprisoned in a body

Figure 6 The Chariot major arcana tarot card

as 'the dead', probably because they saw the soul's life in the body as a kind of punishment. Conversely it was thought of disembodied souls that 'we live their death and we die their life.'[2] The Roman Cicero took this one step further by stating that the ancients accepted that we were born to bodies as a penalty for sins in previous lives.

The philosophers argued over the length of time which elapsed between successive incarnations. St Augustine said that the Greeks believed that there was a conjunction between the same soul and subtle body every 400 years, while Plato said that the time between two births was a thousand years, as did the Roman poet Virgil.

Pythagoras was able to remember many of his former incarnations. He was an initiated son of Mercury called Ithalides in the time of the Argonauts, in which life Mercury granted him the boon of remembering incarnations. He was next incarnated as Euphorbus of Troy. In that incarnation he spoke of his previous incarnation and even knew which species in the animal and vegetable kingdoms he had been previously, although it was expressly understood that a human soul could not return to the body of an animal. He incarnated as Hermotimus and went on pilgrimage to the temple of Apollo at Branchidæ (or the Temple of Juno at Argos). Next he was a Delian fisherman called Pyrrhus, who still retained the memories. And finally he reincarnated as Pythagoras. It was even suggested that he had also been Alce, a beautiful woman of easy virtue, but this attribution by Porphyry is questionable.

THE ELEUSINIAN MYSTERIES AND THE STOICS

The Eleusinian mysteries were practised at Eleusis near Athens, and were most popular in the late Greek period. The foundation of the mystery was the myth of Demeter and her daughter Persephone, who was condemned to spend four months in the underworld every year with the god Hades, and the other eight months in the world of blossoming and beautiful nature. Although it is primarily a nature myth of the seasons, it also symbolized the periodic descent of the soul between lives, with the hellish existence in bondage to the demon king being a metaphor for life in the body.

As in the Orphic and other mystery cults of Greece it was understood that many myths were fables expressing reincarnation ideas, particularly those of gods such as Dionysus and Persephone, which symbolized the destruction of the body and the descent into the underworld, respectively.

The ultimate reincarnation belief in the Greco-Roman world was that of the Stoic philosophers, who believed that the soul was a microcosm of the world which reincarnated after death. Their world view was cyclical, but with the additional factor that they believed that both individual lives and successive cycles of the world repeated themselves identically. The life cycle of humanity was therefore seen as identically recurring periods in which the same souls reincarnated in the same sequence of bodies and repeated identical events.

At the end of each world age all souls returned to the divine soul of the world before starting the next cycle. This meant that life was an endless repetition of the same circumstances, and the idea came to be known as eternal recurrence, which was later espoused by the great German philosopher Nietzsche. Stoicism was an extremely pessimistic philosophy, as it allowed for no growth of the soul during endless repetitive world cycles. It subsequently declined with the rise of Christianity in the Roman Empire.

NOTES

[1] Mead, *Orpheus*, p 153.
[2] Ibid, p 188.

6 · Early Judaeo-Christian Reincarnation Beliefs

The Semitic religions (Judaism, Christianity and Islam) at various times accepted resurrection but rejected reincarnation because they believe that souls are not eternal, and that a new soul is created with each new human life. Their ultimate principles, however, were often politically motivated rather than statements of fundamental beliefs, and therefore made in the interests of the formal hierarchies.

In the ancient Hebrew religion every man, woman and child was accepted as part of the most special and fated race, tribe and family, bound together by the same blood. The organization of the entire race, traditionally composed of 12 tribes, was based on succession from father to son, which however was distorted according to circumstances. For example, when sons sinned, the responsibility was taken by the father. The identity of family and tribe was bound up in these concepts, and individuality in the sense that we understand it had not yet come into being.

That every infant possesses the soul of an ancestor is a primary belief of orthodox Judaism and one of its greatest strengths, and is particalarly special in having some strong reincarnational implications. Indeed, even the Talmud states that Adam was reincarnated as David.[1] But Judaism does not formally accept reincarnation as a belief, despite these historical ties.

Reverence for ancestors is a primary part of the Hebrew religious tradition. Yahweh was God for the Jewish patriarchal lineage, rather than being an individual's god. The 12 tribes of Israel were disenfranchised during their bondage in Egypt, but after the Exodus they identified more strongly and with greater focus upon their ancestors and the purity of their struggles. It was expressed by the later books of the Old Testament through the idea that God's love could not be terminated by death, which implied some kind of belief in an afterlife, and hence resurrection.

REINCARNATION VERSUS RESURRECTION

Towards the time of Jesus Christ more apocalyptic writings appeared to present the influences of other Middle Eastern sects which accepted reincarnation and resurrection beliefs, until it became accepted by some that a prophet would arise from the Hebrew people who would establish a kingdom on earth which resembled the resurrected domain. The Jews subsequently awaited a universal resurrection of the dead, a concept which provided the atmosphere in which Jesus arrived with his controversial teachings.

The life, death and resurrection of Jesus Christ is one of the most profound mysteries in history. Certainly the concept of the Christ arose from a conflux of cultures in which ideas about reincarnation and resurrection were many and varied, but it is necessary to accept that attitudes towards reincarnation at that time and in that place were profoundly different from what they are imagined to be from our present perspective. Indeed, Christ taught Nicodemus that one cannot enter the Kingdom of Heaven unless one is born again of the water and the spirit.[2]

After the Crucifixion, Christ appeared to a number of his disciples on Easter Day, 50 days later, at the Feast of the Pentecost in Jerusalem, they experienced the coming of the

Holy Spirit. The gospels tell of Christ reappearing with his stigmata, eating meals with the disciples and asking Thomas to touch him, but also of his rising in 'a glorified state' which was not physical, but heavenly.[3]

Christ did indeed rise again in spirit rather than in body. In the Acts of the Apostles, it is reported that Paul heard Christ's voice announcing his presence but saw only a blinding flash of light, which he understood as a resurrection appearance. What is the difference between a resurrection and a vision? It is very difficult to say. Most people at that time thought resurrection meant a dead body physically rising from the tomb, and the disappearance of Christ's body seemed to confirm this tradition. However, the legend of the empty tomb discovered after the Crucifixion probably dated from at least 25 years after the event, and could have been created to support the belief that Christ became a quasi-divine power, sitting on the right hand of God.

In subsequent centuries, as Christianity came to be more and more powerful as a religion and a political force, the significance of the resurrection took on very potent energies indeed. The early Church Father Origen (ca AD 185–254) taught reincarnation and the transmigration of souls, and believed that souls came into the world reinforced by victories or defeats from previous lives, which was characteristic of the Gnostic, Platonic and Orphic beliefs which underlay his Christianity.

Origen's beliefs were eventually declared pagan and condemned, but not until the second Council of Jerusalem in AD 553, some 300 years after his death.[4] At that time the Christian Emperor Justinian formally rejected reincarnation, and his Council of Constantinople stated: 'Whoever shall support the mythical doctrine of the pre-existence of the soul and the consequent wonderful opinion of its return, let him be anathema.' Justinian supported the materialist doctrine of a literal Kingdom of Heaven on earth which prospered and became all-powerful. This attitude was popularised by the clergy, who wished to increase their temporal power.[5]

Reincarnation concepts pervaded early Christianity, but there was a shift of meaning from Platonic beliefs in the immortality of the soul to the resurrection of the body. The difference is that in resurrection, by the divine intervention of God, the whole individual is recalled to life, rather than an immortal soul reincarnating in a new body, which is not a revolutionary event.[6] Christianity portrays the patriarchal world view that God created man as a mortal creature, and man must therefore entreat his God to grant further existence beyond the present life. This distinction leads towards a materialist rather than a transcendent philosophy, as we have seen in the history of Christianity.

THE SECOND COMING OF CHRIST

The Second Coming of Christ was understood as the raising of all the dead, body and soul, at the beginning of a messianic age. Literally, the dead would rise from their graves to take their places in the world. This belief led to the Roman Catholic prohibition of cremation of the dead, which continues to this day. The biblical view is that resurrection is the attainment of a garment of light rather than the reincarnation of the physical body, but this is forgotten in the fervour of belief. The judgement of the dead would occur at the time of the Second Coming, and the resurrection of the body would be dependent upon the proper exercise of faith and righteousness, which constitutes the primary morality of Christianity.

As the second millennium approaches, many await with anticipation the Second Coming of Christ, the end of the world prophesied by John, the Last Judgement and the resurrection of the righteous. The belief in reincarnation is directly opposed to this doctrine of reward or punishment after death. In the view of such people, all souls are branded as either good or evil, so that when the resurrection occurs at the end of the world, only the good souls will rise again. The rejection of a system of checks and balances through incarnations was considered evil in itself. These doctrines and the denial of soul to animals leads to the implication that humanity is at the apex of evolution and above the animals, which is one of the most destructive influences of Christianity.

As for the idea of reincarnation, many basic issues remain to be resolved within the context of Christianity, since many

Christians do believe in some sort of reincarnation. The denial of the immortality of the soul raises the question of how a soul is created for every new baby born in the world. It also pinpoints the fundamental difference between Western and Eastern religious beliefs. Eastern religions correlate the conditions into which one is born with the karma acquired over many past lives, but the Western view requires a sense of fate in accepting the will of a God who carries ultimate power (omnipotence) and knowledge (omniscience) over everything in the world.

The primary difference is that in the Eastern view one takes responsibility for one's life and the possibilities for modifying that life through transcendence, and in the West we believe that God is responsible, which relieves us of the necessity to consider our actions and absolves the individual of the ultimate responsibility. The Christian 'forgiveness of sins', and especially the Roman Catholic idea of confession and absolution, is a powerful doctrine, but is mainly interpreted in the purely personal context of moral behaviour, which can be used to excuse or condone sinful activity. It must be left to the judgement of the individual which of these two views lead to the more just morality.

NOTES

[1] Walker, *The Woman's Encyclopedia of Myths and Secrets*, p 848.
[2] John 3: 5–6.
[3] Hick, *Death and Eternal Life*, pp. 173–5.
[4] Campion, *The Great Year*, p 294.
[5] Hick, *Death and Eternal Life*, p 298.
[6] Ibid, quoting Oscar Cullman, p 180.

7 · THE THEOSOPHICAL MODEL OF REINCARNATION

Reincarnation may be experienced through dreams, fantasies, guided imageries, hallucinations, trances or hypnotic regression. The quality of the experience depends upon one's level of consciousness. Those with greater awareness will remember past and present lives which express higher being, while those less developed will experience inferior ones. The karmic mechanism, and it is a mechanism, requires multiple levels of consciousness in order to function. We experience our karmic life as following its own unique destiny and gravity. Sometimes we can relate to it, and at other times we cannot. But we recognize that we must deal with it now despite that.

There are many levels of awareness. Contact with altered states of consciousness promotes the assumption that higher is necessarily better, an assumption which is often not true. A basic understanding of the meaning of the levels of the psyche is essential for interpreting reincarnation experiences. One of the most popular models for describing levels of consciousness is the esoteric model, which originated with Plato and Pythagoras, and variations of which were promoted by the Theosophists – Alice Bailey, Rudolf Steiner, Edgar Cayce and many others. According to this model, an individual is composed of a series of bodies, from a dense physical vehicle to finer and higher spiritual levels of being. The primary difference between the variations is the number of bodies in each scheme. The basic four levels are the physical, emotional, mental and spiritual (*see* figure 7); but there are often subdivisions or higher levels of awareness which extend towards unity with the godhead, here shown as levels 5 to 7.

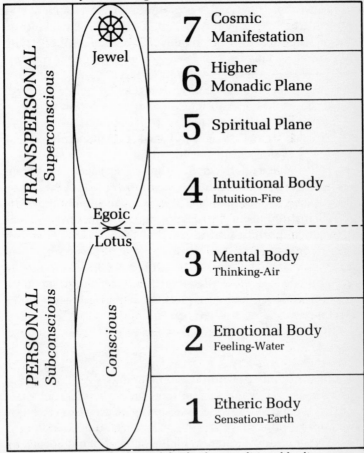

Figure 7   Four-body model. The four traditional bodies are surmounted by three higher transpersonal levels of being.

We all contain the entire complement of bodies, each of which has certain specific functions and limitations. We sense the world through the physical body, our feelings through the emotional or astral body, ideas through the mental body, and higher reality through the spiritual body. The terms used to identify the various bodies, however, vary from doctrine to doctrine.

All four bodies come into being and become one during gestation, but their influences are felt at particular times of life and reflect the archetypal stages of human development. We first identify with the physical body, then we develop an emotional body as our personality, then a mental body with the learning of language and self-expression, then a spiritual body as we acknowledge and understand the world beyond our personal reality. Each body influences a different aspect of our being, yet all are required to combine to form the whole. The relative emphasis we place upon each body determines our character, defines the areas we over- or undervalue in our lives, and sets our karmic agenda in life.

Each body has a relative density and reincarnates at different rates. In order of density, the sequence towards finer bodies is: physical, emotional, mental and spiritual. The denser the body, the more restrictive the laws governing its action. Physical laws are more confining than mental laws – we cannot fly, for example, but we can imagine that we can. Some of us live primarily through our ideas, others through our bodies, and we are all needed to make the world function. But the laws governing the movement of physical bodies are more restrictive than the laws governing feelings.

THE PHYSICAL BODY

The physical body is bound by time and physical laws. It is created in gestation and reincarnates in two ways: it interacts with the environment by drawing energy from food and oxygen in complex chemical processes, and it reproduces. We consume air and food from our environment, which provides our body with energy and chemical raw materials. Specific parts of the physical body continually wear out and are

50

replaced. Our bodily systems, composed of glands, organs, bones and other elements, have durations of less than a human lifetime. Hair falls out and is replaced by new hair, nails grow longer and organs are revitalised, but only to a point. The cells with the longest lives are those in the brain, which last virtually an entire lifetime. All physiological functions interact with the environment and depend upon the air, energy and food available.

The processes of growth and renewal are balanced by processes of decay. When the forces of renewal are equal to or stronger than the forces of decay, the body is healthy. When the forces of decay predominate, illness and death inevitably result. Health is affected by the quality of the environment and by the immune system, the function of which is to protect inner from outer, and to maintain renewal. Impure food, additives, pollution, pesticides, ozone depletion, acid rain, nuclear contamination, food irradiation and a host of other dangers all affect our bodies by penetrating our physical systems and increasing the stress on our immune systems.

The physical body is engineered to maintain optimal health unconsciously. We do not need to think about our bodily processes such as breathing, supplying the body with blood or digestion, they function automatically. In this sense, our physical body is therefore unconscious and automatic.

THE ETHERIC AND ASTRAL BODIES

Reproduction transmits genetic material from parents to children. Many families trace their heritage back hundreds of years, although all humans carry the entire evolutionary process back to the first life. Hereditary physical characteristics, attitudes, ways of being and emotional patterns reappear within the same expanding family over many generations.

The processes of genetic inheritance and environmental interchange combine to create a living human organism during gestation. A series of bodies come into being, each of which has a specific function in the adult (*see* figure 8).

At conception the spiritual germ unites with the hereditary stream to produce the cellular body. After about four weeks

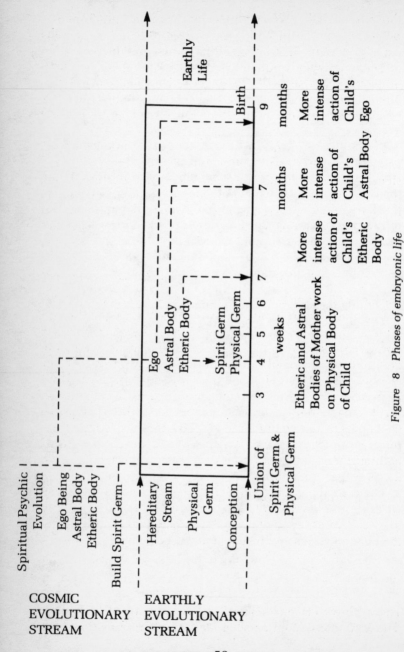

Figure 8   Phases of embryonic life

the etheric body, the architect of physical and formative processes for the incoming ego, links with the developing embryo, deriving instructions from the surrounding world.[1]

The etheric body guides the embryo through a succession of evolutionary stages from one-celled organism to modern human. It carries our instinctive level of being, which includes biological functions such as organ formation, reproduction and dietary dynamics, as well as survival urges.

Just before birth the astral body is derived from planetary and stellar realms and joins the physical and other bodies to signal the arrival of consciousness and the creation of the personality. The etheric and astral bodies are dominant in early life and wane in importance as we age, until both lose most of their formative influence at puberty.

THE EMOTIONAL AND MENTAL BODIES

During our lifetime the two major bodies are the emotional and the mental. The emotional body – created during childhood with the personality as its vehicle – carries the way we act, see ourselves and behave. It contains learned responses to family environment, the set of values within which we are raised, our emotional self-expression and the subpersonalities which are components of the self. Traumatic influences in childhood, identified by Freud as primary components of our psyche, are contained in the emotional body, awaiting reactivation and release through life events which evoke them. The emotional body surrounds and permeates the previous, lower bodies, yet has power over them.

The mental body is created during maturity and is the way we think, our ideas about the world, our beliefs and our ability to communicate with others. The mental body is affected by the ideas of others and by the patterns of the world.

THE HIGHER-LEVEL BODIES

The intuitive or spiritual body transcends the other bodies, which are considered personal. It guides our transition from the personal to the transpersonal domain. The spiritual body is symbolic of the Christ-consciousness or Buddha-nature inherent in us.

The higher-level bodies are planes of being which extend beyond mundane individual experience into realms of pure spirit. On these levels the soul comes into contact with higher intelligences of the universe. These higher formative levels are correlated with Brahman, Vishnu and Shiva in Hinduism, Buddha-nature in Buddhism, the realm of the Holy Spirit in Christianity, and the angelic realms in other religions. The soul craves to return to these higher realms, in which it reunites with the godhead. The material world is understood by the Tibetan Buddhists as an illusion created by mind incarnated into a body, and not a true reflection of the godhead.

The succession of bodies is often symbolised by the seven chakras, which are energy centres located along the spine, from the base chakra to the crown chakra at the peak of the forehead (*see* figure 9). The chakras are energetic organs of the levels of being and gateways of consciousness. The endocrine glands are modulated by them. The transmutation of spiritual energy to physical being is also affected by them. The seven major *chakras* are expressed on the outer levels by the planets or by

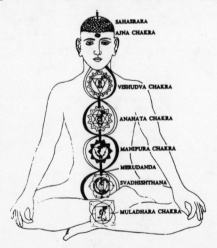

Figure 9   The Chakras

the rays which carry the energies of the planets on an esoteric plane.

Everyone has all four bodies, but the extent to which they are recognized, accepted, worked with or focused upon varies from person to person. There is an obvious hierarchy from dense to fine, and from material to spiritual. The choice must be made by everyone. The true meaning of reincarnation involves the discrimination of focus in life and, by extension, the discovery of the focus of previous and future lifetimes.

NOTES

[1] Jocelyn, *Citizens of the Cosmos*, pp 25–7.

8 · RUDOLF STEINER AND KARMIC RELATIONSHIPS

Behold the fire, behold the smoke; what man turns into fire through his spiritual activity are spirits that he liberates at his death.

Bhagavad Gita

Rudolf Steiner (1861–1925) created a unique body of work which lives on many decades after his life in the Anthroposophical movement. He used his unusual skills of psycho-spiritual observation within a scientific foundation (he called it 'spiritual science') to explore old and new territories of the world and the psyche, and brought together these disciplines into a unified world picture which included architecture, medicine and agriculture.

Steiner was influenced by the great German philosopher Goethe, whose theory of the metamorphosis of plants led him to the concept of a metamorphosis of consciousness, about which he believed people needed to be informed. The idea of the metamorphosis of plants is that within the seed lies the enfolded essence of the eventual tree, and life for the tree is an unfolding of that seed within an environment which will modify its evolution. In many ways Goethe's idea anticipated the concept of the gene. The idea of ascent – that there is a continuity of life forms throughout nature enacted within the individual, which anticipated Jung's idea of the collective unconscious, was also a legacy of Goethe which Steiner incorporated into his world view.

During his dramatic life (buildings he designed in Germany were destroyed during his persecution by the Nazis in the 1920s), he dedicated himself to the description of a spiritual science, in which reincarnation was a fundamental idea. He realised that the true spiritual science had been obscured by the materialist-mechanist scientists of his time, and formulated the idea which is now common among physicists: that the universe is more like a great thought than a great machine. He believed that thought is not merely a mechanical/chemical adjunct of being, but rather is the creator and governor of the realm of matter. This contrasted with the views of almost all the natural scientists of his time. He strove to explore and formulate the governing psycho-spiritual laws and rhythms which are the foundation of life and the key to our destiny in the universe.

The primary principle of reincarnation according to Steiner is the Eastern idea of *ātman* as the 'spirit man' within us. Physical phenomena are merely the expression of spiritual deeds, and beings that appear to us in material form are the outward sheaths of spiritual beings, all reflections of the *ātman*. To penetrate deeply into the natural processes, objects or beings of the world is to discover the active, spiritual principles underlying them. Steiner considered reincarnation a primary mechanism of which it is necessary to become conscious in order to understand and integrate universal laws. Other great minds of modern times, such as Goethe, Nietzsche, Wagner, Emerson, Montaigne and others agreed with him,[1] despite opposition from both the Christian religion and the scientific establishment. Steiner could not accept that spirit was obsolete, but rather believed that it was the essential foundation of spiritual science.

In contrast to Oriental views of reincarnation, however, where the *ātman* passes through repeated incarnations which could be characterized as circular and repetitive, Steiner understood it as a spiral process which, although repeating, ascends upwards through stages of purification and mastery beyond the earthly world. Indeed, he saw this spiralling ascent of the evolution of consciousness being reflected in and connected with the genesis of Christianity. In defence of this unorthodox viewpoint, he reminded students of Christ himself, who said that his spiritual brother John the Baptist had previously been the Jewish prophet Elijah.

Steiner grew up with spiritual perceptions which he later tested and questioned profoundly, but his unique way of seeing the material world from the viewpoint of the spiritual world was the foundation of all his ideas. He abhorred any form of spiritualism or mediumship, however, and although he was briefly associated with the Theosophical Society in its early days he felt its methods and attitudes degraded the higher spiritual. He was pained by the Society's move towards the occult, and left soon after 1911 to found the Anthroposophical League.[2]

To Steiner, the spiritual world was the real world, and he discovered a kind of mathematical logic which pervaded spiritual principles. The basic axiom of his remarkable investigations into reincarnation was that what was then termed the unconscious mind derived from the memories of the race or species was in reality an expression of the principles of karma and reincarnation. This distinction remains relevant, even after the discovery of the genetic code, because the incarnations of the soul follow a different path from genetic characteristics, in that they may jump from one genetic line to another, unlike hereditary characteristics which cannot. In a sense Steiner explored the spiritual world in the same fashion as Freud explored the world of the unconscious, although he did so by looking inward rather than outward.

SPIRIT INFORMS MATTER

Spirit informs matter and guides the process of life through countless natural transformations, such as the periodic replacement of cells within the body, the circulation and purification of fluids and blood, and the impact of diet, digestion and evacuation. On the biological level, our bodies change almost entirely every seven years. But Steiner believed that we must investigate the workings of the architect of the construction, not the construction itself. This architect is the spirit, and the spirit is associated with the element fire. Fire is thus the boundary between the perceptible, material world and the etheric, spiritual realm that is no longer perceptible.

Fire is the only element which can be apprehended inwardly, so it has a twofold aspect. Both ancient and modern spiritual science proclaim fire to be the first stage at which matter becomes soul. Fire builds the bridge or gateway between the outer material world and the inner soul world. We see objects in the external world because of light, but we cannot see light itself. Light makes everything visible but cannot itself be seen. The passage from water to air to fire to light is the passage from the outward, perceptible, to the invisible, spiritual, etheric realm.

Through our thought processes we create formative matrices which define both our physical bodies and the less dense bodies which survive our death. Steiner called these matrices the etheric forces which must be consciously moulded through our growth in life, guided by a spiritual thought-force which is our ego. These forces are in turn interwoven with our memories and together carry a cosmic life pattern or signature which constitutes the karmic forces of our soul.

From the moment of conception the soul is bound up within a new body, but by the end of childhood, at around the age of seven years old, we begin to free ourselves from the dominance of the body as our growth processes begin to peak and then stop. The spiritual energy moves from its attachment to the physical to new areas, particularly the development of consciousness. Even childhood illnesses act as keys to this process, in neutralizing the dominance of the physical body and forcing consciousness to emerge.

Simultaneously, as the etheric forces are gradually withdrawn from the body, the body itself begins to deteriorate gradually through life. In a sense, this is an inverse dynamic:

as our spiritual consciousness grows, so our body deteriorates. Our ultimate goal is to identify with our higher-level body (the soul) which can transcend the laws of the physical domain as it enters the higher worlds. We have an individual etheric body, but it is woven into the fabric of the thought world. The spiritually enlightened individual is very aware of the necessity to balance these forces of spiritual growth and physical reversal to maintain an equilibrium. Thus Goethe and Steiner agree that the maintenance of health is a delicate balance between the opposing forces of the physical and the spiritual.

The body mirrors psyche and spirit, and within its vocabulary each bodily organ reflects a particular aspect of soul development. For example, the stomach reflects the digestion of emotions, while the heart is the centre of love and the brain is the organ of thought-life. The body and spirit follow a parallel and interconnected course in life until death, at which point the physical decays and the spiritual begins to follow its own laws.

In addition, there are elemental beings (aspects of our lower nature) which inhabit us and wish to be released by our activity; otherwise they remain within us until death. Some elemental beings are led back to the higher elements through our activity in the world, while others are not. With the right knowledge, we can build a crossroad for elementals if we want to. The elemental beings which do not return to the higher worlds remain with us through successive incarnations. Objects are often also enhanced by the elemental beings which animate them. By looking at a person or special material object and understanding its true nature, the elemental being animating it is released.

Through wisdom we liberate elemental beings at our death; through materialistic attachment to the world of the senses, we tie them to us and force them into our world to be reborn again with us. During waxing moons spiritual beings of the lower realm rise into a higher realm, while during the waning moon corresponding spiritual beings are bewitched into lower realms, so that order will prevail. Bright and cheerful people continually liberate beings who are enchained by the waning moon. These beings enter them again, but are released through serene soul disposition and inner contentment. For those whose soul mood releases during the waxing moon, the spirits return to higher worlds at the death of the physical body.

The physical body consists of all our material substances and forces, as well as processes of growth, renewal and chemical transformation, whereas the etheric body, our formative body, is the architect of the physical and governs our interaction with the formative world of the cosmos around us.

There is also a third body called the astral body. Since all material of which the earth is composed originated in the stars and conveys the limitlessness of the cosmic spheres, the astral body is the carrier of these influences and is related to the subduing and ordering of the two lower bodies, limiting the concentration of the organism to physical growth alone. It is the matrix of our developing consciousness. These astral influences also correspond to the mechanism of astrology and govern its impact upon our being, psychology and life. They reverberate with the image of the whole in the stars and together form an interactive feedback system which we can use to further work through our karma.

The interaction between these three bodies and the spiritual ego happens throughout life and explains the genesis of our being on earth. When we sleep and our physical body rests, the formative body comes into its own in reorganizing it, and the astral body disengages itself in order to draw new influences from the surrounding world and the universe beyond. We subsequently integrate them through acts of reflection, with the ultimate result of deepening consciousness. Steiner even says that these two life histories are of equal importance, not only during life but also in our existence between death and rebirth.

COSMIC HUMANITY AND THE GUIDES

Steiner believed that the spiritual movements of his time were higher octaves of previous developments and groups of people in history. He felt that Madame Blavatsky was inspired by the Rosicrucian movement of the 13th–15th centuries – it was only 600 years later that Rosicrucian ideas could be understood by the people. Just as the Rosicrucians did not adequately define karma and reincarnation (indeed they were only being formulated in Tibetan Buddhism at the same time), so Madame Blavatsky was also unable to do so. For this reason, Steiner speculated, she drifted towards Oriental forms of theosophy and abandoned her formerly Christian ideas. He felt the need to complete this integration of Eastern and Christian theologies through his ideas about reincarnation.

Steiner stated that the Buddha would return as the Maitreya Buddha 5,000 years after Gautama's lifetime. In the intervening period a succession of bodhisattvas would appear again and again on earth, but none would reach the rank of Buddha. This is the highest expression of Oriental occultism and religion, but he identified a spiritual inflow which was in operation to help develop human consciousness in the present and future. This would act through Oriental concepts such as karma and reincarnation to reveal spiritual laws.

The great individuals who have influenced the spiritual life of our world should really be referred to not as personalities but as individualities who pass through many earth lives. We should listen to those beings who, in previous earth-lives, prepared the way for the great ones, such as St Paul, Raphael, Michelangelo and Leonardo. An example is the prophet Elijah, who proclaimed that everything in the world develops because of a divine ego, which casts rays into the individual 'I' and then unfolds its power in the world. He was a herald of the coming of Christianity and its higher principles. Steiner claims that Elijah returned in the being of John the Baptist, whose role was to act as herald for Jesus Christ, and who forced people to look into their own souls to find the divine within. Both Elijah and John were animated by the same being.

This being further incarnated as the Renaissance painter Raphael (1483–1521), whose work expressed a profound understanding of the mystery of Golgotha, and who was born on Good Friday. Raphael expressed a jubilation at the power of Christianity at a time when it was fragmenting, and announced it through paintings such as the *School of Athens*. Steiner's radical interpretation of this work was that it showed Paul coming among the Greeks and professing the glory of God who died on the Cross, rather than depicting the great philosophers in argument, which is its traditional reading. He saw Raphael as expressing a new impulse in Christianity through his work, which was later to have a profound effect upon Goethe. He saw the same soul living through Elijah, John the Baptist and Raphael, each time responding to the effects of earlier causes and taking them higher and higher in understanding. The same being later incarnated through the great German poet Novalis, who resurrected the Christ-idea through his writings, expressing what Steiner calls a 'living theosophy'.[3]

REINCARNATION RHYTHMS

Steiner felt that there was a rhythm in the reincarnations of great souls, and that parallel streams of incarnations have directed our spiritual history. He considered the rate at which a soul reincarnated, and what determined that frequency. In the earlier stages of humanity's development incarnations were quite far apart, possibly thousands or hundreds of years, which meant that in the intervening periods the soul remained immersed in the spiritual, with short intervals in earth life. As humanity had gradually liberated itself from the density of the material towards the fineness of the spiritual worlds, so incarnations have occurred at an increased rate, and shorter interim times have been needed in the spiritual realm.

Steiner identified three stages in human evolution as phases of reincarnation frequency: an ancient stage of a germ of individuality; a middle stage of increased individuality; and a last, present stage, in which humans experience themselves in human form but with a desire to unite with the spiritual worlds.

Throughout a sequence of incarnations certain laws are in operation. First, there is an alternation between male and female from incarnation to incarnation. Secondly, as souls tend to individuate they are attracted to like souls, and therefore groups choose to incarnate together. Such contemporaries signal their inner significance and the similarity of their quest to each other in order to unite again.

Steiner saw that we are affected by our collective history

stretching back to the origin of the earth and beyond into prior planetary-level embodiments, and that we carry this history within us.

THREE MEMORIES WITHIN

While in earth consciousness, there are three categories of memory which live within us. The first is the unfolding of individual consciousness day by day. In order to 'possess' this consciousness, however, we must wake up and use our senses as spiritual instruments through which to guide the physical body. This awareness is conditioned by our earthly life with its specific laws and functions. But when we die to pass on to another life between death and rebirth, our body decays and we are only soul and spirit. We therefore have different instruments at our disposal through which to contact our essence. That which we owe to nature drops away, and the more profound, deeper and ethereal being within us is called into action. In this state, our everyday consciousness, which we have spent a lifetime perfecting, falls away and is of no use. We have the option either to persist in connecting our memory of life with our disposable body or to link it with a higher vehicle within us which survives the physical body, such as the etheric body.

It is the time between lives, during which we are living in the memories of the etheric body after our physical body has decayed, that we see the tableau of our entire life, the Last Judgement described by religions such as those of the Egyptians and Tibetan Buddhists, as well as the Christians. According to Steiner, the memories of our life are inscribed in the life-ether permeating space, remaining there for ever (the akashic record of the Theosophists). We carry with us an extract of this and previous lives into our next incarnation.

This brings us to the second principle, which is that our individual inner experiences of consciousness become part of the universal ether and are retained for ever within the ether body.

The third principle is that the sum of our actions as expressions of our personal morality and soul are stored within the astral body. After the physical body has decayed, and the etheric body which contains remnants of consciousness has disappeared, the astral body remains with its memories of deeds inscribed within the astral cosmos. This connection with deeds from life are passed on to further lifetimes through our karma, our moral focus and becomes an encyclopedia of our behaviour towards others.

THE FOURTH LEVEL OF BEING

Beyond our physical, etheric and astral bodies, there is a fourth level of being, the earthly 'I'. This passes through many incarnations preserving karma and previous life memories, awaiting the faculty of comparison and rectification when it awakens through spiritual practice. The 'I' is uniquely earthly, owing its being entirely to life experience rather than either of the longer-term memories (etheric and astral). Similarly it is our function as humans with a spiritual 'I' to remember, understand and work through our karmic responsibilities and to participate in the evolution of spiritual being on earth. In a sense, by coming into conscious being, in accepting our karmic responsibilities, we become truly human and connect with our true spirituality and the collective purpose of all humanity in spiritual growth and evolution. What makes humans sublime is our ability to be aware of and live with these responsibilities and through them to come closer to the godlike and the spiritual being from which we arise. The more our thoughts and actions reflect the selflessness associated with karmic beings, the more our individuality flowers and our power grows. In this way we come closer to what Steiner called the 'Spirits of Form', beings of higher hierarchies which determine human evolution itself.

In previous times it was our spiritual leaders who accepted this responsibility for all human karma, and lived and died for the collective spirit, but now we ourselves are required to bear the burden. In this way Steiner relates human progress to the mystery of Golgotha and the Christian spiritual life.

He identified the stages during gestation when the various bodies described above join together to create the cosmic human. Figure 8 (page 52) shows this sequence, from the tangible physical essential karma derived from our genetic heritage and joined in the instant of our conception to the spiritual energy of the integration of sperm and egg, to the joining of the etheric, astral, and finally the personality at birth. We gather these bodies into the whole which is our human birthright, and translate them into cosmic humanism by our thoughts and consciousness of the karmic requirements we carry and which define our lives. This process, which in ancient times constituted initiation, is now a responsibility for many of us in this life and in these troubled times. Steiner dedicated his life and teachings to the transmission of this image of the cosmic human sensitive to karmic necessity.

NOTES

[1] Wachsmuth, *Reincarnation*, p 7.
[2] Steiner, *Earthly and Cosmic Man*, pp 12–13.
[3] Ibid, pp 103–14.

9 · THE LAST JUDGEMENT AND EVENTS BETWEEN LIVES

When the process of dying is complete, our physical organism begins to fall away and deteriorate. As this happens, the etheric body is relieved of its responsibility and can transmit images of the life process and their inner meaning without being impeded by physical desires. This explains why people who have had near-death experiences report seeing their lives pass before their eyes in an instant. This is what the ancients called the 'Last Judgement', and it is extremely important because this instant replay determines the quality, timing and karmic significance of our next incarnation. What had previously been human consciousness, limited by its earthly life, is freed to return to the cosmos and transformed into a cosmic consciousness.

THE LAST JUDGEMENT

A most fascinating description of this critical and powerful time of spiritual renewal is investigated by Rodney Collin in

The Theory of Eternal Life, in which he analyses the similarities between the Egyptian, Christian, Islamic, Greek and other Last Judgements and assesses their significance.[1] He developed a graphic image of the life process which corresponds intimately to the central reincarnation idea – that life is a circle.

This is quite a revolutionary idea because the process is rarely seen in that way, even by those who espouse reincarnation or spiritual ideas. We generally understand life only as the period from birth to death, indeed as a straight line between the two. This is the inexorable path of life, with event following event, in the familiar cause and effect sequence which governs all things. In reality, it is necessary to incorporate an additional stage of the process, because the gestation time, from conception to birth, is also extremely significant for our development. As we saw in Chapters 7 and 8, this time is not only important but critical in understanding our whole life process from a spiritual standpoint.

One important variant idea Collin includes is that time is not additive during our lives, with each hour or day being equal to every other, but rather that it changes according to a logarithmic scale (*see* figure 10). At conception, when sperm and egg meet and the biological development begins, the process of life proceeds at a very fast rate, virtually molecular rate, close to the speed of light. Changes happen almost instantly as cells divide and join, diversify and become complex. As we become more complex during gestation, and further through life, our rate of development gradually slows, until at death it stops.

Collin discovered that the scale grades our entire life in such a way that it reflects the energy and information flowing into and out of our human form as we age. For example, young children move fast, have a rapid metabolism, digest food almost instantly and want more, perceive things quickly and become bored immediately, yet they sense the passage of time as taking for ever. As we age, all biological, emotional and mental processes slow down, and we gradually become aware that time is moving ever faster and becoming more condensed, year by year. Collin calculated that the passage of time for a seven-year-old is approximately ten times slower than for a seventy-year-old, yet ten times faster than for a new-born infant. Therefore, instead of the creation of our physical body during gestation being about one-hundredth of our life process (nine months as against over 77 years), using the logarithmic scale it occupies one-third of the whole, leaving the remaining two-thirds for the time from birth to death.

The second third of our life lasts from birth, when we gain our personality and develop it within the family system, until the age of seven years old, and in this time we create an emotional body. As the Jesuits believe, at seven years old our personality has in essence been accepted and developed. The last third, from the end of childhood to death, and during this time we create a mental body within the outside world. During maturity we combine and integrate body with personality, project this combination out into the world and work out our various possibilities. While this last stage is typically when we go to school, develop a world view, create family for ourselves and solidify our existence in the physical world, some people use this time to awaken the soul, a process analogous to the initiation described by Steiner.

Throughout our entire life process our metabolism (the rate at which our body processes food, oxygen and perceptions) and rate of development slows down, much like a spinning top slows down and gradually stops after being launched. Collin graded the process in such a way that each successive stage is ten times longer than the previous stage and one-tenth of the next (gestation is ten lunar months long, childhood 100

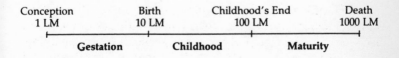

Figure 10   The Logarithmic Time-Scale of Life

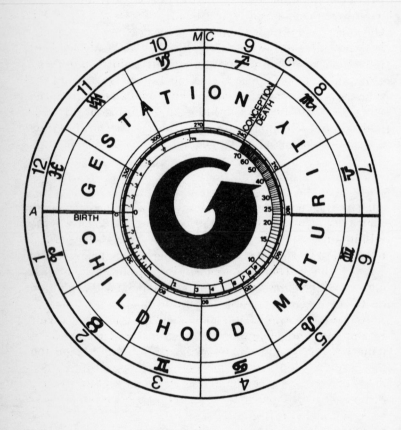

Figure 11 Life-Time Scale. The circular process of life can be correlated with the sequence of astrological houses and signs.

and maturity 1,000). As that rate slows down with age, so we perceive that life accelerates more and more, until in old age it moves so fast that we cannot keep up with it at all.

What is unique about Collin's scheme is that when complete, the line of life from conception to death can be wound around a circle so that conception and death coincide (*see* figure 11). Our energy and karmic inheritance at the moment of conception is all potential, as life has not yet begun, while at death all our potential has been translated into actuality, and life is done; the circle is complete. Similarly, the burst of energy of the sexual integration at conception is like the burst of energy at death, when the soul is liberated and sloughs off the physical vehicle, which is left to disintegrate. This energy connects death and conception, and as such it works outside time.

THE TIMELESS DOMAIN OF THE SOUL

At the moment of death, the soul enters a timeless domain which we call eternity. As Collin expresses it, 'All points within time are equally accessible, or rather, they are all related, not by time, but by the intensity of the energy which informs them.'[2] The death moment is a distillation of our life, and reduces experiences to their essence, and the agony of death echoes the ecstasy of conception.

Accepting that conception and death are one, and since the information and energy of these critical instants creates a pattern which is unique in time and space, Collin realised that the absolutely unique karmic energy signature liberated at death can only be accepted or receive its imprint in the same instant as conception, creating a circular process which loops back in time to the beginning.

Plato probably derived the idea of eternal recurrence from the Egyptian mysteries, and it was elaborated upon by Nietzsche. According to Plato, after death the soul journeys through eternity, through various pasts, presents and futures, to find a new womb in which to incarnate, choosing its new life according to the residue of experiences of the last life. The paradox is that most souls are so mechanically attached to their lives that they will always choose to repeat the life that has just passed rather than risk the possibility of attracting a new life which may be in some way inferior to the old life. Through our life we should have improved upon and evolved beyond the karma we were born with, but this is rarely the case. The result is incarnation stagnation. If we arrive at the Last Judgement, the process which occurs between lives, with full understanding and memory of our life (and lives), we have an open choice, but most souls cannot imagine or conceive a different life and choose what is familiar.

The judgement is essentially the same, whether it is Tibetan, Egyptian or Christian. Collin quotes the vision of the 3rd century Christian St Macarius of Alexandria, in which his soul was guided by its guardian angel for three days, ascended to God for the adoration, experienced the pleasures of paradise for six days, descended again, and then wandered in hell for 30 days, awaiting its final judgement. In the Tibetan Buddhist tradition, the disembodied self or soul has many visions and experiences in the world between worlds, the purpose of which is to locate a new body in accordance to the record.

The process between lives always includes glimpses of heaven and pleasures as well as journeys through unimaginable hells and tortures, visions of light and darkness. This opportunity to choose is unique in the between-life state in eternity, because once the soul has attracted a new body in which to be conceived and born, the next opportunity for choice will not be until the next death, after a lifetime of being fixed in incarnation. It is therefore appropriate that there is a equation between conception, death and judgement, which together close the life process into a circle.

But, where does the journey between lives take place in this scheme? Most religions agree that a period of time elapses between the death of the physical body and the re-entry into a new womb and the beginning of the next life, and this period ranges from 18 to 49 days. The dimension in which the journey takes place is beyond ours (or at a right angle to ours) and lies in another circle, tangential to the first, intersecting at the moment of simultaneous death and conception. For as in the ancient metaphor of the ouroburos snake biting its tail around a circle, the death and conception points are one.

Collin surmised that the duration of this crucial missing period between lives, which is not included in the ouroburic circle of life, is logarithmically as long as the rest of our existence put together. Due to the compaction of time in the supersensible world, however, it seems to happen in an instant. Since we are pure spirit during this process, the fineness and speed of our vibrational rates prevents us from being in a body in the traditional sense. We therefore live in a world of the spirit, which could be a molecular world.

It is the between-lives existence of which those who have had near-death experiences have seen the first glimpses. In Tibetan Buddhism it is the 'primary clear light' of perfection in Buddhahood, while in the Egyptian religion it is identity with Osiris, and in Christianity the ascension to the throne of God. In this state our karma is compressed, refined and assembled so that it can be seen and interpreted as an experience according to the language of the religious symbols with which we were raised in the former life, guided by the masters of the spirit.

The vision is intense, extended, and so cosmic in dimension that it is the true revelation. It is like the billions of internal and external images received in a lifetime, or many lifetimes, compacted into an instant. It is truly the most powerful and immediate experience possible, and justly occupies its place at the forefront of all major world religious practices. Indeed a glimpse of this moment constitutes the awakening of Buddhism, the enlightenment, or the 'death before one dies' of the Sufi masters.

It is justly understood that the power of reincarnation lies in this domain, where we have a unique opportunity to make the choice for which our entire life, or sequence of lives, has prepared us. It is a chance we cannot afford to miss or misinterpret.

The judgement is a playing out of all sides of our nature, strands of our genetic code or streams of our karma, and a weighing of the parts or bodies of ourselves against each other simultaneously, in order to find the common denominator or overriding spiritual vision which will determine our next incarnation. The drama in this sense is an interior one, played out against a backdrop of cosmic dimensions, but hopefully directed or reinforced by a spiritual guide, guru, priest or lama

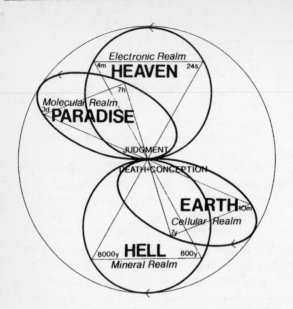

Figure 12 The Four Worlds. The four circles are dimensions of existence. The visible cellular world and the invisible molecular world intersect horizontally at the instant of conception and death. The lower circle is the hellish mineral realm, while above is the heavenly electronic realm of pure spirit. (After Collin, The Theory of Eternal Life.)

outwardly, and by a superhuman being such as Christ, Osiris, Yama or Ahura Mazda inwardly. We are shown the way by our tutelary divinity, if we have one, and in each case this being represents the universal spirit, the guardian of the electronic realm in which this all happens.

The weighing of the soul, which is central to the drama, also happens in each religious context, whether by the Lord of Death, St Michael or Anubis. We are judged before the soul passes through a metaphoric river of forgetting, like the River Lethe in Greek myth. We are weighed against our accumulated karma, the stored memories of our life and its unique requirements and actions, the tablets borne by our soul, or the feather of the Egyptian scribe Thoth. We are judged by our inner qualities, not the amount of wealth we have accumulated, or the honours we have been bestowed or the outer deeds we have accomplished. We are weighed against our personal truths, our way, our *dharma*. And in this instant we are consigned to the next body awaiting our soul impression which the judgement has determined.

THE AKASHIC RECORD

Many occultists, seers and Theosophists postulate the existence of an akashic record, a store of information of all lives, to which certain psychics, spiritual masters or clairvoyants have access. It was mentioned by seer Edgar Cayce to explain how he knew so much about people, past and future. He described a great library where there were books about people's lives, recording everything in great detail. This record had accrued from the subconscious of all individuals in history. With the appropriate prayer and humility, he claimed to be able to go there at will and simply take out the appropriate book and read from it. It sounds like a virtual library in which he could browse, and he supports this view by saying that it was to the spiritual world what a movie archive would be to the physical world. He believed that anyone able to travel on the astral plane could gain access to this universal record. It is this akashic record or its equivalent which contains the psychic karmic records upon which we draw in our important judgements between lives.

THE GROUP REINCARNATIONS OF EDGAR CAYCE

The 'sleeping prophet' Edgar Cayce (1877–1945) left records of over 140,000 telepathic-clairvoyant sessions. Central to a perspective on this massive body of raw material was Cayce's belief in reincarnation. He believed that not only is reincarnation an integral part of reality, but that prior incarnations are often indicated as a source of illness in this life. Steiner also accepted this idea in his Anthroposophical medicine.[3] Cayce was able, through further inner questioning and investigation, to facilitate a cure in people who were ill.

Cayce also remembered some of his own past lives. He stated in trance that he had been a swashbuckling Cornishman named John Bainbridge, born in 1742. Bainbridge had landed in America at Chesapeake Bay, very near where Cayce spent the later years of his life and founded his healing centre at Virginia Beach, Virginia. Bainbridge was an Indian scout and struggled with Indian tribes in America. He eventually lived at Fort Dearborn, near the modern city of Chicago. When Fort Dearborn fell to the Indians, Bainbridge attempted to save a large group of men, women and children by taking them down the Ohio River on a raft, pursued on both sides of the river by Indians. Many of the settlers died of starvation or exposure and Bainbridge himself died saving a young woman's life.

Cayce's dramatic past life as Bainbridge became relevant 150 years later, when a group of more than 20 of the original Dearborn settlers reincarnated around him in Virginia Beach. When Cayce moved there in 1925, many of the people he had attempted to save during his life as the scout Bainbridge were already there. This 'soul group', as Cayce called them, was to remain supportive throughout his life.

Cayce discovered that many of the health afflictions of people in his soul group were caused by conditions at or around Fort Dearborn in their previous incarnation. He identified a case of tuberculosis contracted in the dance halls of Dearborn and a form of polio suffered as a result of malnutrition caused by the Indians, to name the most dramatic instances. His ability to identify past lives and their circumstances led to cures in both the above cases and provided people with direction in life – a firm, spiritual path to follow.

NOTES

[1] Collin, *The Theory of Eternal Life*, pp 66–73.
[2] Ibid, p 9.
[3] Wachsmuth, *Reincarnation*, pp 200–90.

10 · PSYCHOLOGY, BIOLOGY AND REINCARNATION

The spirit is born, lives and never dies.
    Mrs Smith, Guirdham, *Cathars and Reincarnation*

In modern times many people have tried to explain or modernise concepts of reincarnation using the methods of science, but with limited success. This has recently involved explaining it through genetics. Apart from a few radical scientists, there remains a basic denial of the reality of the psyche and the spiritual domain within science. The probable reason is that there is no way to measure the existence of the subtle body, psyche and soul, but this will always be the case. But some adventurous and brave thinkers have attempted to integrate these concepts into their views of the world.

CATHARS AND REINCARNATIONS

The British psychiatrist Arthur Guirdham read medicine at Oxford and was a Senior Consultant in Psychiatry. He has presented the concept of reincarnation in many of his books on healing, psychic factors in mental illness and reincarnation itself. In 1970 he wrote a fascinating book called *Cathars and Reincarnation*, which was the record of a process of discovery by one of his woman patients, whom he called 'Mrs Smith', who received impressions in waking consciousness of a previous life as a Cathar heretic in 13th century France.

The Cathars (also called the Albigensians) were a heretical Christian sect which existed in the Languedoc region of the Pyrenees in south-western France until they were virtually eradicated in the early 13th century.

They were civilised humanists with strong anti-Catholic convictions, who developed a following in Provence before spreading into the Languedoc region near the town of Montsegur, where about 200 Cathar priests were burnt for heresy. These priests, who could be either male or female, and were called *parfaits*. They received a unique sacrament known as the *consolamentum*, sometimes even on their deathbed. They were chosen at birth, and lived lives of purity and sacrifice through fasting, meditation, chastity and good works. They abstained from all animal foods except fish. It was also possible to become a parfait after having married and had children, and indeed this was recommended.

Guirdham initially saw Mrs Smith in 1962. She came with a history of quasi-epileptic attacks accompanied by visions since childhood, and presented symptoms of which the most prominent was that she regularly had bad dreams which woke her at night screaming so loudly that it disturbed her husband and their neighbours. She had already had these dreams for 20 years. Guirdham checked her for traces of epilepsy but found none, and after his interview with her, her dreams stopped and never recurred again. In an intriguing synchronicity, Guirdham himself had also suffered from 30 years of recurrent nightmares involving a strange man entering his bedroom in the night. After his session with Mrs Smith, these also stopped.

In the course of his continuing sessions with Mrs Smith, Guirdham happened to mention that he had been to the city of Montsegur in the south of France, the historical centre of Catharism, and wondered whether she knew the area at all.

She had not been there, but had recently read a book about French medieval history which mentioned the Cathars, a subject which she had found absorbing. She was shocked at the synchronicity, and at the apparent connection with the Cathars.

In the following two months Mrs Smith bombarded Guirdham with references to the Cathars, including the information that a manor house centre he frequented in southern England, which was owned by Buddhists, had been founded by someone associated with the Cathars some seven centuries earlier. He began to suspect that she had psychic powers of which she was not aware. A friend of Guirdham's also suggested during this time that he himself could have been associated with the Cathars, partly because of his irrational, deep dislike and distrust of Roman Catholicism and partly because of other strange attitudes of his, which were similar to those of the Cathars. His belief in what he called religious dualism meant that he did not accept that Christ actually incarnated, but that he remained pure spirit, a view also held as central by the Cathars and Rudolf Steiner. The web was tightening.

Over a period of years, Mrs Smith wrote down fragments of her dreams, and they contained addresses, episodes, isolated place names and recollections of a former life in a women's community in the Middle Ages, as well as memories of poems sung to her by a man named Roger, whom she loved. Striking incidents included a powerful horror whenever the city of Toulouse or the Cathedral of St Etienne were mentioned. Subsequently Guirdham discovered that St Etienne was where the Inquisition's nearest chapter to Montsegur met. He was also able to identify a character who often stood next to Mrs Smith in her medieval memories as a certain Pierre de Mazerolles, who had been implicated in a murder in Cathar times, and had been reported to the Inquisitors. In her repetitive dream he had come to her for shelter from the agents of the Inquisition, who were chasing him, and it transpired that he was her brother in those times.

Mrs Smith was able to recall strange and exotic customs which were peculiar to the Cathars, information she was

Figure 13   The Cathar symbol which resembles the astrological sign of Pisces.

extremely unlikely to have had access to in her present life. Indeed, some of her insights gave Guirdham unique views of the Cathars which contradicted the current knowledge of them, but which were subsequently proven to be true. She remembered Cathar robes as blue, whereas historians generally agreed that they were black. Obscure references in the Bibliotèque Nationale in Paris confirmed her memories.

She drew from memory a strange silver symbol which she maintained Cathar parfaits wore to fasten their girdles and which Roger wore on a ring on his thumb. It was like the astrological symbol of Pisces, with two upwardly curving lines crossed by a horizontal (*see* figure 1). Guirdham discovered references to this symbol, and also found that she was correct in her memories of the Cathars' unique customs. She continued to be accurate on a score of details of life in those troubled times. She was even able to remember and write down the original spelling and form of early troubadour poems and songs. Her knowledge of these ancient forms was unique and Guirdham found that when her memories or dreams contradicted the prevailing historical records, she almost invariably turned out to be correct. She also filled out her memories by describing and naming subsidiary characters, many of whom it was possible to identify through historical records from the area.

What is most extraordinary is that Guirdham eventually realized that, although he had no memory of having been in medieval France at the same time as Mrs. Smith, realized he had himself in person been there too, and that an entire group of Cathars had, through his research and relationship with Mrs. Smith, come together again after a gap of 700 years. They had taken part together in great tragedies and tests of their reincarnation beliefs, which were an integral part of Cathar religion.

THE COLLECTIVE UNCONSCIOUS

The theories of the Swiss psychologist Carl Gustav Jung support the ancient idea that there exists within us an encoded history of our species. Jung believed that we possess access to the 'collective unconscious', a layer of the psyche beneath consciousness containing the instinctive drives, habits and behaviourial patterns we share with all humans. The collective unconscious lies beneath, and was created before, the personal unconscious, which is composed of our childhood experiences.

Jung believed that the collective unconscious was a source of much creative vitality and imagination in humanity. Its images are expressed primarily through art, dreams, music, fairy tales and myths. We have access to them through dreams, visionary experiences, fantasies, guided imagery or hallucinations. Jung never discovered the source or method of transmission of the collective unconscious – only that it existed and could be proved to exist.

Jung's work is compelling because the structure of the unconscious in modern humanity contains the beliefs and behaviour patterns of early times, as do our dreams. The deeper layers of the psyche are structured by historical or prehistorical patterns which Jung called archetypes. These are inherited structures, unconscious patterns which affect conscious experiences. Jung accepted reincarnation beliefs as expressions of the collective unconscious and believed that they utilize the structure of archetypes within the human psyche. The psychology of the unconscious studies and uses these principles and their application as a therapeutic tool for working with people to foster individual growth.

GENETIC CODE AND INFORMATION TRANSMISSION

If Ducrocq, Hoyle, Narlikar and Costa de Beauregard are right, then the universe is just as well organized and functions just as precisely as a DNA molecule in the nucleus of the cell, and just as we have succeeded in discovering the genetic code, we should also be able to find the astronomical code. The communication of information is not restricted to living organisms, it is also an integral part of the universe, as are matter and energy.[1]

Increasing evidence from physicists and biologists supports the concept of reincarnation as a common phenomenon in the physical world, although it not identified as such. While reincarnation seems very complex and its mechanisms unfathomable, at the infinitely small molecular level of reality, its principles become crystal clear.

Molecules have lifetimes of a fraction of a second. Since we are composed of molecules, we have a molecular body which is continuously dying and being reborn. Each day, we experience the death and rebirth of thousands of molecular bodies. There must be a mechanism which transmits the memory of experiences, feelings, ideas, spiritual cravings and other attributes to successive molecular bodies. Molecules transmit information in an instantaneous and highly efficient manner, and molecular reincarnation happens constantly within us.

The workings of the genetic code, our reservoir of inherited form, instincts and behaviour patterns, functions in a way which was formerly explained by reincarnation. Genes determine the creation and functioning of the biological being, but we also have access to the collective psyche of humanity. Investigation of the genetic code has determined that we use only a small proportion (less than 10 per cent) of the vast amount of information stored in our genes. The purpose and function of the remaining information is unknown. Similarly, only small areas of our brain are used in normal activities. Does it not seem logical that the 90 per cent of unused genetic code might store the record of all our ancestors back to the primeval slime.

But reincarnation beliefs go far beyond genetics. Heredity is transmitted only in linear succession, from parent to child. Reincarnation transmits some aspects of life influences to the next incarnation, which may be to another family, racial stock or time in history. Reincarnation is not bound in time and linearity like heredity. After death the soul does not necessarily reincarnate immediately – it may do so at any time – nor will it necessarily reincarnate ahead in time because it may also move backwards into the past. Your next incarnation may be thousands of years ago and your last incarnation might be hundreds of years into the future. No one-way arrow of time exists in reincarnation. Indeed this mechanism may be the device through which karmic development is activated. When one evolves within a lifetime, one may progress forwards in linear sequentiality although the issue of whether the future is truly more evolved than the past remains to be decided.

REVOLUTIONARY BIOLOGY

The current mechanist-materialist scientific view is that the genetic code is the only biological intelligence which creates form, transmits information and guides the life process.

The biologist Rupert Sheldrake has proposed a new way of looking at biology. His *hypothesis of formative causation* states that every organism possesses, in addition its physical and chemical systems, a non-physical morphogenetic field (a form-generating field) which organizes the creation and continual coming-into-being of its biological system. Individuals of each species have access to a field of information shared by that species. Behaviour patterns, attitudes, ideas and instincts are shared by all members of the species and indeed organize inheritance and the creation of their form. The morphogenetic field interacts with and amplifies the genetic code to produce individuals, but it determines more than just the primary physical qualities described by genetics.

In an early experiment, it was found that each successive generation of rats learned to negotiate a maze more quickly, apparently demonstrating that the ability to learn is transmitted by heredity. Some years later, Sheldrake tested a separate family of the genetically identical rats which had not learned the maze. They were able to negotiate the maze as proficiently as the last rats involved in the experiment. This implied that there was some kind of transmission between individuals of the same species alternative to and transcending heredity. Sheldrake called this mechanism *morphic resonance*.

He observed a similar phenomenon in crystals. The initial formation of a crystal from a liquid medium takes a long time. Once one has been created, however, similar crystals can be generated more quickly thereafter. Learning is therefore transmitted to the entire species, and not only through inherited characteristics.

The hypothesis of formative causation was tested in 1986. A group of American schoolchildren were taught a series of Japanese children's songs. One was an ancient favourite which had been sung by Japanese children for centuries, while the others were composed specifically for the experiment. The ancient song was found to be easier for the children to learn because many others had learned it and sung it in the past.

The collective knowledge contained within and transmitted by the morphogenetic field changes and grows after the hereditary transmission of genes at conception. Sheldrake's theoretical method of transmission comes close to the traditional reincarnation model, with the primary difference that reincarnation involves the transmission of qualities that far supersede the biological to include the other subtle bodies. Moreover, reincarnation transmission can pass backwards or forwards in time rather than in a purely linear time sequence like morphogenesis.

Genetics on the biological level, morphogenetic fields on the experiential level, archetypes of the collective unconscious on the psychological level, and spiritual enlightenment on the spiritual level. Not only do these four quite different concepts echo ancient reincarnation ideas, they also provide us with a powerful illustration of the ways in which various forms of reincarnation operate within us.

NOTES

[1] Landsheidt, *Cosmic Cybernetics*, pp 56–7.
[2] Sheldrake, *A New Science of Life*.

11 · EXPERIENCING REINCARNATION

The recent growth in interest in reincarnation has led to the material available on the phenomenon becoming a minefield of prejudice and hearsay, because people have often written about and believed whatever they wanted rather than what they could prove. An investigation of reincarnation therefore requires us to use a combination of modern knowledge and common sense. For instance, it is important to make a distinction between the karmic history of a soul as it passes through successive incarnations, and personal character traits which are passed on from one generation to the next through biological generation, although in practice it is extremely difficult to do so.

Many individuals have character traits in common, as they are the archetypal core of our individuality. Modern psychology is based upon this hypothesis. People may think that they are remembering other incarnations when they are actually experiencing archetypal layers of the collective unconscious within themselves. The transmission of character traits does not constitute reincarnation. Evidence for reincarnation depends upon access to deeper levels of being within which a person's life destiny are expressed, rather than more superficial qualities which are carried by the personality alone.

Memories of the events of our life are fragmentary. When we think of it as a whole, we are besieged by random memories, some from early childhood, others from adolescence or from last week. There is rarely any order or form to them. It stands to reason that memories of past lives are going to be similarly fragmentary at best. And once they have been discovered, it is difficult if not impossible to prove whether they are valid or not.

We have both a conscious and an unconscious memory. Events which we cannot clearly remember today may emerge into consciousness next week or next year – we remember them but we do not know that we remember them. We contain memories which are not always available to consciousness, but which await discovery. Memories of past lives similarly reside within the unconscious in most people, awaiting discovery.

It is interesting and compelling to see the ways in which people experience reincarnation in their lives. One of the primary methods is the direct memory of previous lives which emerges in certain people, which has then been verified. Ian Currie's book *You Cannot Die* presents a number of cases which are extremely persuasive, despite the fact that it is virtually impossible to ascertain how they came about. He discusses a case seen by a Dr Stevenson of a full-blooded Tlingit Indian who, just a year before he died, told his niece that he would return as her son. To verify this, he said that her son would have two scars on his body similar to those which he himself had as a result of surgical operations. Eighteen months after his death, she gave birth to a son, who duly had marks in exactly the same places. When the child was thirteen months old and just learning to talk, he spontaneously said, in a Tlingit accent, 'Don't you know me? I'm Kahkody.' Kahkody was the tribal name for the dead man.

Over a number of years and in spontaneous situations, the young child identified various members of his family by name. He was able to recall information about places and events which he could not have known. But by the time he was nine years old, memories of his previous life began to diminish, then stopped completely. By the time he was 15, he remembered nothing of his former life. Dr Stevenson found through his research with many such cases that it is characteristic for the early childhood memories of previous incarnations to disappear at about the age of six, although they can be retained into adult life.[1]

Hypnotic regression is another important way for incarnation memories to surface. The difficulty in these cases is that it is necessary to research the historical details that emerge. And, to eliminate any suspicion of complicity, it should be someone obscure but historically verifiable. It is obvious that not every previous female incarnation can have been Cleopatra, which represents more of a wish fulfilment than a possible reincarnation reality. Currie mentions that in an analysis of 1,500 cases of reincarnation regressions, the average time that had elapsed between the past death and the present birth was 52 years. Since records more than 75 years back are not always easy to check, this presents problems of identification.

A woman spontaneously regressed during a meditation session went back in time and found herself with her family standing at a square in a north Italian city, entering a horse-drawn wagon, on the way to visit her father's parents at their large and prosperous farm in the countryside. When asked when it happened, it was clear that it was 1533. In the hallway of the farmhouse was a circular staircase, on which she remembered playing make-believe, and familiar smells evoked childhood memories of hidden places and strange adventures. The family was shown into a large, panelled room surrounded by portraits, with a grand table set for a formal lunch. When she looked at her parents, she knew her father was a tall, dark and pale doctor from Berne, Switzerland, and her mother was weak and physically delicate, and she felt distant from both of them. Her grandmother sat at the head of the table, directing the servants, and she recognized her as her equivalent grandparent in this life. As her blond grandfather came late into the room, everything came alive and he brought a new energy into the gathering. Throughout the meal the adults talked about the food, business affairs and other boring things – at least they seemed boring from an eight-year-old's viewpoint. The meal was endless, and after a period of time she became bored and came back to the present.

What is interesting about this story is that it was spontane-ous and not arranged in advance, nor was the subject hypno-tised. It is also strange that the paternal grandmother in previous life was the same as her present grandmother, and that her father in the regression looked vaguely like her first husband in this life, who was also a doctor. Was it suggestion? Is this a fantasy? It is characteristic of such experiences that the borderline between reality and the new world opening up is tentative at best.

A case mentioned by Currie is that of George Field, whom hypnotist Loring Williams regressed at the age of 15. The boy remembered a life as an illiterate, reclusive farmboy named Jonathan Powell in North Carolina, who was murdered by Civil War soldiers in 1863, some 85 years before Field's birth. When he was taken to the town in which Powell lived, he was able to identify local personalities of the time, children's names, homes and their appearances, and other relevant material which he could not have known. But no official record of Jonathan Powell existed, and property records of the time did not mention him or his grandmother Mary Powell. Articles were published, but no information came to light until George Field received a letter from a grand-niece of Jonathan's, who commented at length on his life, and said that he had ultimately been killed by the Yankees in the war.[2]

Helen Wambach's experiences with regression show some apparently strange consistencies which on reflection turn out not to be so strange. She analysed the social classes of thou-sands of people she regressed and found that only 10 per cent were previously born into upper-class families, while the vast majority, some 75 per cent, were workers, which would tally with the class divisions of previous ages. Similarly she found that the frequency of regressed former lives seemed to fit with the smaller world population in former times.[3]

Dr Wambach also discovered a phenomenon which seems to support many of the religious beliefs in reincarnation. She began asking subjects who had died in earlier lives why they were born, and also why they had died. Many appeared to know why they were born and up to 95 per cent had at some level chosen their parents or life situation. When the choices were wrong, they also knew that and could then end their lives prematurely. When asked why they chose to be incarnated again, a majority answered that they needed the possibility to advance their personal development, but also said that their physical lives were largely unsatisfactory. When asked what was the primary issue in the new incarnations, most said that it was the environment which gave a prospect for development and evolution of potential.[4] It is in many ways not surprising that testing regression cases seems to bear out the attitudes of religions such as Buddhism and Hinduism, in which these ideas are central to their beliefs about reincarnation.

Most people cannot remember their past incarnations, but some yogis and spiritual masters have demonstrated prodigious abilities in this regard. The Buddha is renowned for being able to remember all his past lives; indeed in Buddhism such recall is a prerequisite for liberation from the need to reincarnate.

The unconscious quality of most past-life memories is verified by the experiences of Rudolf Steiner and Professor Ian Stevenson of the University of Virginia. Both discovered that reincarnation memories were most vivid in young children. As we age these memories become more distant and vague, until they are 'forgotten' completely.

REMEMBERING OUR GENETIC RECORD

Our genes are known to carry a record of our genetic inheritance, but is this evidence of reincarnation? Everyone alive is the result of a 100 per cent successful breeding process. Our parents gave birth to and raised us, their parents created and raised them, and so on to the first humans, to the first life. By definition, nowhere in our past has there been a single failure! Everyone on earth shares a common ancestry and it would seem that we also share many memories in common. In a strictly Darwinian sense, since only the fittest survive, we are the fittest because we have survived.

The population explosion has fostered a misunderstanding of the mechanics of population. That humanity seems almost infinitely diverse is obvious, but if we go back five centuries we find that our common ancestors outnumber those to whom we are unrelated. If we trace the expansion of generations backwards in time, we are confronted by fantastic statistics. Assuming 20 years per generation, a child born in 1980 had 8 million direct parental ancestors in 1500. In 1400 that number becomes 250 million, the approximate population of Europe. The intermingling of the population is more complete than we imagine. Yet, anthropologists have hypothesized that the *Australopithecus* female they call 'Eve' could be the mother of all humanity.

The distorted view of our own uniqueness is compounded by the fact that we imagine the population of the world, even in Roman times, to have been vast, whereas 2,000 years ago Rome itself had only a few hundred thousand inhabitants. The population of the known world of the Romans was not much larger than that of England today.

The implication is staggering. Our heritage is much more homogeneous than we imagine. Even the division into races happened only within the last 15,000–20,000 years. We all have ancestors from the early cradles of humanity – continental Europe, the Middle East and Africa – and ultimately we probably all derive from central Africa. It is no accident that the search for roots is one of the primary obsessions of modern humanity. We are one large family, as disturbing or consoling as that may be.

My maternal grandfather was a genealogist, and passed down to me a circular diagram showing the diversity of our ancestors in the last eight generations. It shows his two parents in the central circle; outside that is a ring divided into four, with their fathers and mothers; then their eight parents; then 16; and so on up to an outermost ring of 128 descendants in only seven generations! The variety of surnames is amazing and it shows how wide the influence of even the narrowest families would be if they were traced and documented. It is certain that we have many more relations around us than we imagine.

OUR HEREDITARY MEMORY

The idea that our hereditary memory contains the panorama of history waiting to be accessed is a sobering and integrating concept. The fact that many channelled spirit guides are Neanderthal or Cro-Magnon primitives may be a reflection of the fact that we all carry hundreds of generations of such ancestors within us, peering through time at us from a closer proximity than is comfortable.

Biologically, each fertilized ovum contains chromosomal information garnered from preceding generations. According to biologists, the quantity of information inherited from our ancestors is present in proportion to the number of generations, in an ever-diminishing ratio.[5] Half of our chromosomes derive from our mother, one-quarter from our grandmother, one-eighth from our great-grandmother, etc. Taking the mechanism back into past centuries, we contain a molecular (or homoeopathic) potency of all of our ancestors, which may help explain how they are so potent, yet indefinable except through exploring our unconscious processes.

The research of Dr Helen Wambach of San Francisco into hypnotic regression reincarnation memories indicates that most of her subjects remembered humble and peasantlike previous existences. Indeed, more than 90 per cent of the past lives her subjects recalled were lived as primitive food gatherers, nomadic hunters, or farmers, and less than 10 per cent recalled aristocratic former lives.[6]

The spirits within us wait for an opportunity to communicate denied them in the recent centuries of Western civilization. Our civilized personalities do not allow the more primitive and essential aspects of our nature a satisfactory means of expression, so they must break through into consciousness in order to be heard. Yet when they do, we consider it madness. Recently the men's return-to-nature and women's goddess-consciousness movements have provided a valid channel for these energies within to surface and receive acknowledgement. Everyone has inherited memories of this vast process in all its richness. As a species we are only now, and only some of us, beginning to realize how to gain access to and take advantage of the wisdom and experiences of the past ages stored within us.

THE PHENOMENON OF CHANNELLING

Channelling is the establishment of communication with beings from other times or dimensions. The tradition of spontaneous revelations of past lives is extensive and has paralleled the popularity of the teachings of channelled beings. As it is not the object of this book to recount such experiences which are abundantly covered elsewhere. However, it is undeniable that the phenomenon is much more powerful and pervasive than anyone would like to admit. It is as common in fundamentalist Christian sects as it is among fringe believers. Psychologists such as William James, C G Jung, Dr Lawrence LeShan and Dr Stanislav Grof have not only accepted the concept of channelling, but have integrated it into their psychological theories.

Channelling and reincarnation have much common ground. Both are powerful tools for attaining wholeness, yet they are also primarily subjective. Evaluating a channelled reading can be as difficult and perplexing as verifying a past life experience. The paradox is that channelling affects many people who would not be expected to believe in it. While there may not seem to be any connection between channelling and reincarnation, a brief discussion of channelling will set it in context.

The Victorian spiritualist tradition brought Eastern religious ideas to the West through channelled material. Theosophical Society psychics, primarily Madame Blavatsky, Annie Besant and Helena Roerich, as well as many mediums, provoked people to investigate the spiritual realm, and as a by-product the public was presented with a deeper wisdom.

Channelling is evocative to people because they want to believe that there is life after death, or that there are ancient beings willing to share their wisdom. And, what better way to experience such a supernatural existence than to communicate with the spirits of the dead, especially recently departed relatives? Although a majority of the Victorian mediums were undoubtedly frauds, the mechanism of mediumship is important to understand because it is an instance of individuals receiving information either from previous incarnations or by tapping the akashic record. And some channelled material is valuable in its insights, in its challenges to prevailing views and in its bizarre projections of the future of the earth.

Many major religions and sects have been founded on channelled transmissions, including Muhammad's revelation of the Koran from Allah, George Fox's vision which became the basis of the Quakers' beliefs, and Joseph Smith's contact with the angel Moroni which led to the Book of Mormon. One could also include John and his reception of the Book of Revelation. Such people are often able to speak in tongues and are either worshipped or condemned for their efforts. Among the most prominent channels in our century are Edgar Cayce, Alice Bailey and Jane Roberts. They and many others have attracted attention from serious people and have been influential in the foundation of the New Age.

Transpersonal psychology owes much to the beyond. Many people do not realize that both Freud and Jung wrote early papers on the occult. They both went through stages of investigating the possibility that channelling, reincarnation and the occult were essential to psychology. Nandor Fodor's *Freud, Jung and Occultism* is a thorough investigation of their writings on occult matters, which includes an analysis of Jung's channelled *Seven Sermons to the Dead*. The source of the modern psychotherapeutic movement developed by Roberto Assagioli, called Psychosynthesis is Alice Bailey's channelled works of esoteric psychology and astrology.

With the popularity of channels, trance mediums and gurus it has become essential to be able to tell whether their material is right for us or an expression of fantasy. One consciously or unconsciously signals to others who may have had incarnations at the same times we did by our taste in art, our religious beliefs, philosophy of life or choice of lifestyle. When we meet people who are attracted by our deepest cultural or religious signals, they can validate our life. Relationships are vehicles for seeing ourselves from the viewpoint of another person, which brings a depth to our own life.

Channelling is another way to make contact with deeper levels of oneself. We will be attracted to channels who evoke in us feelings or information which we deem valuable. Usually people who accept channelling blindly have difficulty accessing their own deeper nature. It is essential, if we experiment with channelling, to identify the quality and spiritual level of the transmission, once it is accepted that the transmission is a valid one.

The parapsychologist Lawrence LeShan investigated many cases of trance mediums who channelled entities and categorized the possible explanations for them. He concluded that what people call spirits may be one of three things: actual spirits as they claim; split-off aspects of the personality of the medium or deeper levels of their own genetic memory; or a phenomenon for which there is as yet no explanation.[7]

To LeShan's three possibilities we must add that they might be the inner voices of our own previous incarnations.

NOTES

[1] Currie, *You Cannot Die*, p 266.
[2] Ibid, p 286.
[3] Ibid, p 312.
[4] Wambach, *Reliving Past Lives*, pp 89–90.
[5] Jacob, *The Logic of Living Systems*.
[6] Wambach, *Reliving Past Lives*, p 181, and Michael Talbot, *Your Past Lives*, p 5.
[7] LeShan, *Alternate Realities*.

12 · Astrological Reincarnation

We have seen that a primary mechanism for transmitting characteristics across successive incarnations is the astral body, and the astral body is the organ through which we take in, assimilate and utilize planetary influences. So what would be more natural than to explore models for determining incarnations which are based on astrology?

The famous British astrologer, occultist and Theosophist Alan Leo (1860–1917) was highly influenced by the idea of reincarnation in his astrological work, and his thinking set the tone for the development of modern astrology in Britain.[1] As a youth he believed that our souls were connected with the stars and thought that it would be seen that astrology was no less than a science of reincarnation – in effect that the two philosophies would be integrated. His astrological work therefore explored aspects of the law of karma, and his book *Esoteric Astrology* described his theories of the karmic essence of astrology. He said:

> To-day my whole belief in the science of the stars stands or falls with Karma and Reincarnation, and without these ancient teachings, natal astrology has no permanent value.[2]

Leo used Indian astrology, with its unusual harmonic subdivisions of the zodiac circle, as the foundation of his astrological reincarnation work, in order to integrate Western astrology with the traditional Hindu doctrine of the transcendence of the soul. This placed less emphasis upon the personality as the outer appearance and vehicle of this higher, inner body, and presented a deeper and more influential version of astrology to the public of his time.

He found that he could see incarnative influences in the horoscopes of many of his clients and revealed to them what they had brought into their current life, but he never developed a way of determining when or what these previous lives were about in any more detail.

RETROGRADES AND REINCARNATION

The astrologer Martin Schulman correlates the movement of retrograde planets (planets which because of the earth's movement around the sun appear temporarily to be moving backwards) with reincarnation.[3] This seems logical because if the natural, forward movement shows the development and evolution of consciousness and life qualities into the future from birth, then retrograde movement symbolizes those influences in us which are moving backwards towards the past, and conversely could potentially symbolize those which emanate in the past and are affecting the present. Indeed Schulman believes that not only do retrograde planets regress back some days, months or years, but they also regress back to previous incarnations, and their movements signal memories of such past lives.

The astrological focus on retrograde movement encourages us to identify and resolve earlier karma which we have carried into this life. Although not claiming to be able to identify which influences are invloved or when they happened, Schulman does accept that magnetic influences from the past have a profound effect upon our psychology and spiritual development in this life. When it is accepted that we may be affected by our past as well as our future, it follows that we may be more strongly connected with times other than the present – indeed not connected closely to the present at all. This would

have a profound influence upon our psychology, and knowledge of this factor would at least allow us to know what it was
that was influencing us so profoundly.

Schulman identifies 'retrograde individuals' as those who
have three or more retrograde planets, any retrograde inner
planets (Mercury, Venus or Mars), or any retrograde planet near
the ascendant and mid-heaven of the horoscope.[4] Such people
tend not to see the world as matter or form, but rather experience it through their spiritual vision – ultimately they experience karmic lessons which entail primitive struggles for
survival until the retrogrades return to forward motion at some
point in life. Traces of such etheric or astral influences transmitting karmic patterns make the planets 'heavier' than usual,
and bring their hosts a greater weight of influence than normal.
Nonetheless, these karmic messages are profound spiritual
keys in life for most of the people who possess them.

ASTROLOGICAL REINCARNATION

The psychologist Carl Jung thought that because astrology and
star lore had been used by humanity for so many thousands of
years the human race had collectively projected much knowledge onto the planets, luminaries, stars and constellations
themselves. This understanding is available and waiting for
those who tap into it, those with the sensitivity and awareness
to recognize it as the great resource it is.

It is only natural that because the planets carry such projected historical influences as well as karmic records, there is
an astrological bridge which links our present life with the
past. I have developed and presented just such a system of
ideas in my book *The Divine Plot: Astrology and Reincarnation*.

Testing an astrological reincarnation theory in our own lives
initiates an examination of our needs and appetites, historical
interests, literary tastes and behaviour patterns which proves
to be extremely revealing. We carry the entire coded history of
the human race within us, but our access to this great cornu-
copia of knowledge, experience and understanding is often
either blocked, vague or sporadic. It may be activated by

unusual emotional states, life crises, deaths around us, sexual experiences, psychic episodes or psychedelic drugs, which have the character of breakthroughs, rather than being within the usual range of our life experiences. Similarly, while our dream life originates at profound levels of being, as we wake the clarity vanishes almost instantly, as though the genie summoned by the magic lamp of the unconscious is a mirage which inevitably disappears.

Our higher self speaks to us, but such moments are rare, tend to be fleeting and are difficult to sustain. How is it possible to bring the wisdom of previous ages, which we have within, and our higher spiritual reality, which seems to lie above us, into the reality of the outer form of our lives? What is the connection? How substantial is it?

The relationship of waking consciousness to the lower and higher levels of being is analogous to the narrow spectrum of visible light within the broad range of electromagnetic energy – the tiny segment of the entire range of energies which we consider consciousness is minuscule, but most people consider it to be the whole. As we have seen, both transcendent Eastern religions and the Western spiritual tradition point to the fact that an individual life bears the same relationship to the total fund of experience: it is but a glimmer of a very rich whole. It is as though we only glimpse the invisible dimensions below and above us through a dark glass, or else mislead ourselves into thinking that they are really not worth the effort to gain access to them through meditation, spiritual practice or opening ourselves up to the unknown within.

In order to understand our place within the scheme of things it is essential to create a symbol system which will bridge the gap between reincarnation as a history of the soul and our personal life and traits, with which we can identify. Astrology is the natural and obvious choice for such a linking system, as it has always carried aspects of both the mundane world and the spiritual path. In order to understand why, it is necessary to preview the basic assumptions of a new, relativistic view of astrology.[5]

Modern science has proposed that most aspects of appearance, health, temperament and behaviour are determined by

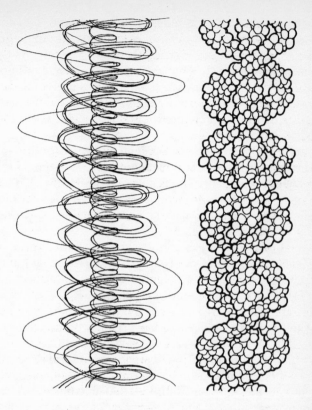

*Figure 14   The Spiral Solar System and the DNA molecule. The sun
moves through space in its orbit around the galactic centre,
drawing the planets with it in a spiralling symphony. The form of
this spiral is similar to the DNA double helix molecule.*

the genetic code, DNA, which exists within every living cell.
The double helix of DNA is a highly intensive and efficient form
of information storage which is continuously available to all
organic life forms. What is evident upon examining models of
DNA is that its shape is very similar to the shape of the spiralling
solar system in time (*see* figure 12).

Physicists identify resonance as a mechanism by which
similar patterns of energy exchange information instantane-
ously, whether they are in the same room or across the

universe. Particles moving in similar patterns transmit information both ways, faster than light. Psychologically, when others are 'on the same wavelength' as we are, they resonate with us and understand what we are doing, wherever they are in relation to us. The process of resonance is central to astrology because the movement of the planets resonates with the DNA molecule commanding biological processes within every cell.

A surprising fact is that the structure of DNA is virtually identical from person to person. The variations which make such profoundly different appearances or temperaments are relatively minor in comparison with the similarities that exist. Only the different sequences of the information in DNA differentiates us from one another, and indeed from other primates or other life forms. Therefore, we all have access to the same universal biological information bank, but choose to use it in different ways. It could easily be that the DNA strand within each cell operates like a receiver as well as a code, not only carrying its own genetic information, but also receiving and transmitting other information at the higher and lower levels of the spectrum of being. The brain and nervous system are devices which interpret and act upon this information.

Astrology is the correlation of the movements of the planets in the macrocosm with the information of the genetic code in the microcosm. This was identified by early philosophers in the phrases 'As above, so below' and 'The macrocosm is the microcosm'. According to this analogy, we carry the life history of our species encoded within the DNA of every cell in our bodies, and through the form of the DNA we also have a resonant receiving mechanism tapping into all humanity, a species memory, the akashic record or what Jung called the collective unconscious.

We are capable of accessing information beyond our personal genetic memory to include our species memory, into which we occasionally tap unconsciously and, with training, consciously. A symbol system such as astrology allows us to merge the information carried by planetary cycles with our biological, psychological and spiritual being. One of the ways in which this information can be made available to us is through reincarnation related to astrology.

Reincarnation is a memory of past lives, but to discover which past lives at which levels of the spectrum of life, we must combine spiritual heritage and modern scientific biology into a continuous scale stretching from the primitive to the profound. This is important because we all contain traces of planetary life through the minerals of our body, animal lives from our pre-human ancestors (the reptilian cortex of the brain), proto-human lives from our simian and proto-human ancestors, mythological identities (the gods and goddesses within us from the early mythological eras of human history), historical lives from our ancestors in the historical era, family lives from our grandparents, parents and immediate family, psychic lives from those around us from whom we take and have taken feelings and psychic impulses, and higher vibrational lives from the molecular/spiritual level of being of the planetary or galactic soul. We are only conscious of participating in our family and psychic lives, but these other dimensions are available to us as well.

As Eastern religions teach and Steiner postulated, we are part of the spiritual hierarchy of the universe. We are intermediaries between the physical and the spiritual, and we carry within us samples of all ranges of human behaviour from the most primitive to the most sophisticated. Thus we have bodies, senses, appetites and behaviour which we share with animals, yet we also have spiritual aspirations which transcend the animal kingdom and the world of three-dimensional bodies. We utilize and live through our instinctive nature in sexuality, hunger, respiration and sports, but we must not let it govern us.

REINCARNATION TIME-SCALE OF HISTORY

Our psychological/spiritual make-up is mapped by the layers of historical humanity we carry within, which are symbolized by our previous (and future) incarnations in time. To determine our previous incarnations, it is necessary to grade history mathematically to correspond to the 12 zodiac signs, each of which corresponds to a developmental stage in human evolution. The resultant time-scale begins with the approximate date for the origin of consciousness, which coincided with the

Signs	
AD 1950	
Pisces	Institutionalism World Wars; chaos and collapse; isolationism
AD 1910	
Aquarius	Scientific; Nationalism Socialism; idealism; science; evolution
AD 1840	
Capricorn	Industrial & national revolutions; capitalism Reformation
AD 1720	
Sagittarius	Renaissance humanism Colonization; enlightenment; philosophy
AD 1500	
Scorpio	Feudal; crusades; medieval; inquisition; magic Monasticism and Cathedrals
AD 1100	
Libra	Dark Ages; Roman law; barbarians East-West synthetic religions & Islam
AD 400	
Virgo	Classicism; Greece & Rome Classical pantheons & Christianity
800 BC	
Leo	Archaic hero-king religion & Hinduism Civilization; individuality; Egypt
3000 BC	
Cancer	Neolithic grain goddess cults Religion; cities; nuclear family; Nippur
7000 BC	
Gemini	Mesolithic tribal cults Language; villages; tanist
14,000 BC	
Taurus	Upper Paleolithic earth mother cults Earth Mother cults; fertility
26,000 BC	
Aires	Paleolithic celestial cults Celestial cults; nomadic; consciousness
48,000 BC	

Figure 15   The Stream of History

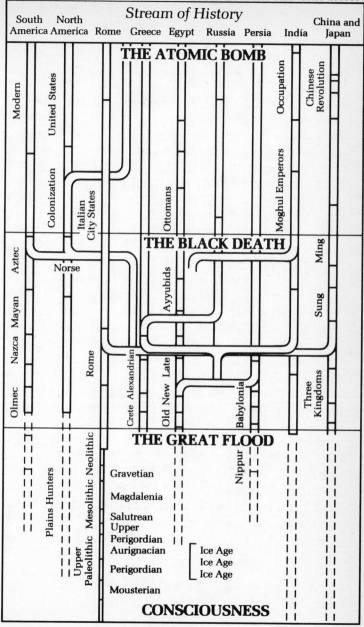

Figure 15 The Stream of History

emergence of our Cro-Magnon ancestors about 50,000 years ago. Before that time the Neanderthals had been highest on the evolutionary chain for the previous 500,000 years. The Neanderthals were short, beetle-browed and did not have language, while the Cro-Magnon were taller, fairer, much more advanced and attained a far superior degree of communication. The Cro-Magnon were the first true humans, who looked and acted like us.

The end of the present era of humanity is taken to be the magical millennium year AD 2000, which describes a 50,000-year historical cycle. 50,000 years is two complete cycles of the precession of the equinoxes, the inexorable backward progression of the earth's axis through the signs of the zodiac, called a 'great year' by the ancients.

The degrees through the zodiac, from the beginning of Aries to the end of Pisces represent particular times in history (*see* figure 15). Each planet in a person's astrological birth horoscope symbolizes characteristics, behaviourial patterns and archetypal ways of being which come into play during his or her life. The time when each planet registers in one's life, and when it is subsequently reactivated, keys off (daily, monthly, yearly, etc.) psychological influences which play their part in creating one's individuality.

Each degree of the zodiac can be correlated with a date in the time-scale, so each component of our personality can be derived from developments experienced by the human race at particular times in the past. We bring the past into the present naturally, often without realizing it. The release of dance or vigorous exercise takes us back to the early Stone Age freedom of movement typical of the Aries time; the pyramids and sphinx evoke the Egyptian Leo time of the pharaohs; while the enjoyment of a Beethoven concerto evokes the Capricornian sense of dominance over nature and the highest human expression of order. Such evocations are constantly with us, form the roots of our lives and inform our actions. The more we understand our historical roots and undercurrents, the richer and deeper the sense of our lives may be (*see* figure 16).

The system uses the positions of the each planet in the horoscope to determine the date of the 12 major incarnations in history, corresponding to the ten planets, the ascendant and mid-heaven. For example, the position of the sun is compared to a table showing the zodiac signs related to dates in history, and its location pinpoints a historical era in which our masculine energy and spiritual orientation was determined through an incarnation. This may range from the self-assertive cave man in early times (corresponding to the Aries time) to the detached Victorian gentleman in more recent times (corresponding to the Aquarius time).

The sun sign is familiar to most people, but the moon and the eight planets are also each resident in particular signs of the zodiac, and they therefore symbolize the other components of our being and also previous incarnations in other lifetimes. The assumption is that each planetary quality in our horoscope in this life contains an analogous time in history from which it derives its influence and character.

Once we know the astrological signs and degrees of each of the eight planets, the sun and the moon in a horoscope, their positions may then be translated into direct dates in the reincarnation time-scale table.[6]

OUR PLANETARY INCARNATIONS

Astrologically, each planet in our horoscope represents an aspect of our nature which has come into being at a particular time in history, determined by the sign of the zodiac in which it resides. Each zodiac sign in sequence represents a stage of human spiritual evolution, and we therefore each carry within us various stages of that process, all striving to dominate the whole. Each planet is a behavioural archetype and is qualified by its specific historical time. Our function is to recognize these historical layers of being which are associated with planets and incarnations, to communicate with them to understand their needs and dynamics, and then to integrate them into the whole of which we are capable.

In our personal life history, planetary influences are identified with people who influence us and the corresponding part of us which identifies with them. For example, the sun is the archetypal father and symbolizes our relationships with him,

LOGARITHMIC TIME SCALE

Degree	Pisces	Aquarius	Capricorn	Sagittarius	Scorpio	Libra
00	Jan 1911	Nov 1841	Oct 1719	●Jan 1500	1109 AD	419 AD
01	Oct 1912	Nov 1844	Mar 1724	Jul 1509	1128	449
02	Jun 1914	Nov 1847	May 1729	Oct 1518	1143	478
03	Jan 1916	Sep 1850	Jul 1734	Dec 1527	1161	507
04	Aug 1917	Aug 1853	Aug 1739	Dec 1536	1177	536
05	Mar 1919	May 1856	Jul 1744	Sep 1545	1192	564
06	Oct 1920	Jan 1859	May 1749	●May 1554	1208	591
07	Apr 1922	Oct 1861	Mar 1754	Nov 1562	1223	618
08	Sep 1923	May 1864	Nov 1758	Feb 1571	1237	644
09	Mar 1925	Dec 1866	Jun 1763	Jan 1579	1252	670
10	Aug 1926	Jun 1869	●Dec 1767	Apr 1587	1266	695
11	Jan 1928	Dec 1871	Apr 1772	Feb 1595	1280	720
12	May 1929	May 1874	Aug 1776	Nov 1602	1294	744
13	Sep 1930	Oct 1876	Nov 1780	May 1610	1307	768
14	Jan 1932	Feb 1879	Jan 1785	Oct 1617	1320	791
15	Apr 1933	Jun 1881	Feb 1789	Jan 1625	1333	814
16	Aug 1934	Sep 1883	Feb 1793	Mar 1632	1346	837
17	Oct 1935	Nov 1885	Feb 1797	Mar 1639	1358	859
18	Jan 1937	Jan 1887	Dec 1800	Jan 1646	1371	881
19	Apr 1938	Mar 1890	Sep 1804	Oct 1652	1383	902
20	Jun 1939	●Apr 1892	Jun 1808	May 1659	1394	● 923
21	Jul 1940	Apr 1894	Jan 1812	Oct 1665	1406	943
22	Sep 1941	May 1896	Aug 1815	Mar 1672	1417	964
23	Oct 1942	Apr 1898	Feb 1819	Jul 1678	1428	984
24	Nov 1943	Mar 1900	Aug 1822	Jul 1684	1439	1002
25	Dec 1944	Feb 1902	Dec 1825	Jul 1690	1450	1021
26	Jan 1946	Dec 1903	Apr 1829	May 1696	1460	1040
27	Jan 1947	Oct 1905	Jul 1832	Mar 1702	1470	1058
28	Jan 1948	Aug 1907	Sep 1835	Oct 1707	1480	1076
29	Jan 1949	May 1909	Oct 1838	May 1713	1490	1094
30	●Jan 1950	Jan 1911	Nov 1841	Oct 1719	●1500 AD	1109 AD

N.B. 0° and 30° of the next sign are synchronous.

Figure 16   The reincarnation time-scale of history

DATES FROM 48000 BC TO 1950 AD

Virgo	Leo	Cancer	Gemini	Taurus	Aries	Degree
811 BC	●3000 BC	6891 BC	13811 BC	26117 BC	●48000 BC	00
758	2905	6722	13511	25583	47050	01
705	2818	6557	13216	25059	46118	02
654	2720	6394	12927	24544	45203	03
604	2630	6234	12643	24040	44306	04
554	2543	6078	12365	23545	43426	05
506	2456	5924	12092	23059	●42563	06
458	●2371	5774	11824	22583	41716	07
412	2288	5626	●11561	22116	40885	08
366	2206	5481	11304	21658	40070	09
●321	●2127	5339	11050	●21208	39270	10
277	2048	5200	10803	20767	38486	11
233	1971	5063	10559	20334	37716	12
191	1896	4928	10321	19910	36962	13
149	1822	4597	10087	19493	36221	14
108	●1749	4668	9857	19085	35494	15
68	1678	4501	9632	18684	34782	16
29 BC	1608	4417	9411	18291	34083	17
10 AD	1540	4295	9194	17905	33397	18
● 48	1472	4175	8981	17527	32725	19
● 84	1406	4058	● 8772	17156	32065	20
121	1341	3943	8567	16792	31417	21
157	1278	3830	8366	16435	30782	22
192	1216	3719	8170	16084	30159	23
223	●1155	3610	● 7976	15741	29548	24
●260	1095	3503	7787	15404	28948	25
293	1036	3399	7601	15073	28360	26
325	978	3296	7418	●14748	27783	27
357	921	3196	7239	14430	27217	28
388	966	3096	7064	14118	28662	29
419 AD	811 BC	●3000 BC	6891 BC	13811 BC	26117 BC	30

Figure 16   The reincarnation time-scale of history continued

with anyone who is fatherly towards us, with men in general, and with the masculine principle in ourselves, and which we project onto others. The sun is also a metaphor for qualities of consciousness, self-awareness and objectivity which we contain and express through our individuality. In history, the sun is a male incarnation reflecting the prevailing attitude to the masculine principle at that time. If we have sun in the sign Aquarius, registering in the late 19th century Victorian era, our father could be quite detached, patriarchal, prudish, idealistic and live very much in our minds and morality, as would the male archetype within us.

The moon is initially our mother, but also symbolizes anyone who is motherly to us, women in general and the feminine aspect of our own nature. She is our feelings, emotional attachments, ability to nurture or support others, as well as the values we hold. The moon in history corresponds to the way we understand this dynamic. An Aries moon registering in 40,000 BC, before nuclear partnerships existed, could indicate an attitude towards emotional attachments which was individualistic, self-motivating and tribal. We could feel spontaneously, respond aggressively to threats and maintain our distance from others, qualities derived both from Aries moon in astrology and from an incarnation as a cave woman.

The positions of the sun and the moon and their relationship to each other show us the make-up of our masculine and feminine nature as well as the potential for their integration. This is also symbolized by the two time periods in history in which these two incarnations registered. If we have within us both a cave woman and a Victorian gentleman, we can see that certain problems of communication and integration could occur. In understanding their relative needs and historical origins, we could at least begin to understand what these two extremely different parts of us are saying. In the same sense if we understand them as two previous incarnations both wishing to communicate with us, we could easily see that it would be advantageous for us to accommodate them, different though they seem to be.

The sun, the moon and the planets are divided into three general categories which represent levels of being within us.

ASTROLOGICAL REINCARNATION

The bodies closest to the earth – the sun, the moon, Mercury, Venus, Mars, Jupiter and Saturn – are the inner, personal planets because they refer astrologically to the way we act, feel and express ourselves, and are usually based upon parents, siblings, family members and friends. We are shaped by qualities derived from people around us when we are young.

The outer, collective planets Uranus, Neptune and Pluto represent qualities derived from the world, such as from friends and foes, the media, political movements and associations.

The personal points are the ascendant (also called the rising sign) and the mid-heaven, which are not planets but rather positions in the birth horoscope corresponding to the sunrise point in the east and the noon point overhead. They describe our personality (the ascendant) and ego (the mid-heaven). The personal points are always in different signs and signify that our personality and objectives in life are archetypally in tension with each other. They show us that our personality derives from an archetypal phase of history. For example the Sagittarius ascendant corresponds to the Renaissance – so such people would try to be Renaissance women or men in their lives – humanistic, optimistic and open to new or challenging experiences. If the mid-heaven/ego were in the sign Pisces, corresponding to the early 20th century, it would indicate a late incarnation, possibly someone highly affected by world history, the media and new ideas and with the lack of formal boundaries characteristic of that sign, and would imbue the ego with such qualities.

It is possible to have each of the ten planets and two personal points in different signs of the zodiac, although in practice this almost never happens. Every person has a unique distribution of planets in signs. Our distribution determines the variety of and intervals between our previous incarnations. Planets grouped closely together imply several incarnations within short periods of time. Planets spread around the horoscope imply broader coverage, a wider range of past life experiences and less concentration. No pattern is inherently good or bad, but it is helpful to understand which pattern describes our past lives.

Each planet represents a type of person which correlates to

109

a past life, and each has its own specific quality and personality types. For example, we all contain all the planets, and therefore all have both the warrior Mars and the feminine moon. But when in history did they come into being and how do these two types relate to each other within us? Each planet and personal point falls in one of the three broad eras of history: Mythology (48,000–3000 BC), civilization (3000 BC–AD 1500) and Individuality (AD 1500–1950). We therefore contain gods and goddesses from the signs Aries, Taurus, Gemini and Cancer; historical archetypes from the signs Leo, Virgo, Libra and Scorpio; and individualized personalities from the signs Sagittarius, Capricorn, Aquarius and Pisces. The warrior in us may be a recent incarnation, while the woman in us is an ancient goddess.

Each planet describes types and incarnations in each of the three eras. The sun represents creator gods, heroes, kings, patriarchs, emperors, popes, lords and presidents, and refers to the masculine archetypes of the father and the wise old man. It describes a masculine incarnation in which we expressed our conscious and objective being, had a dominant spiritual direction and led others.

The moon represents the creator goddesses, earth mothers, lunar deities, earth goddesses, queens, empresses, heroines, significant women, matriarchs and mothers. It is an incarnation in which we expressed feminine archetypes of the great mother, the wise old woman, expressed our unconscious and subjective feelings.

Mercury represents Titans, twin gods, intellectuals, thinkers, orators, authors, critics, mystics, alchemists and magicians. It is an incarnation in which we developed our mental faculties, learned to communicate, concentrated on business and expressed flexibility and breadth of interest.

Venus represents fertility and grain goddesses, deities of the arts and music, goddesses or gods of love, artists, musicians, architects, poets, playwrights, dramatists, lovers, actors or actresses, courtesans and young women. It is an incarnation in which our aesthetic and creative nature was embodied, when we had powerful loves and our appearance was historically derived.

Mars represents gods and goddesses of war and strife, heroes, conquerors, generals, politicians, amazons, politicians, explorers, tyrants, martyrs, athletes, violent people and young men. It is an incarnation in which and through which we aggressively showed individual qualities, self-expression, separateness and tension.

Jupiter represents spiritual and procreative gods and goddesses, prophets, religious founders and leaders, philosophers, psychologists, sages and saints. It is an incarnation of expansive and wise archetypes, in which our religious and spiritual life was developed.

Saturn represents paternal, rigid and orderly gods and goddesses, material deities, scientists, great thinkers, doctors, mathematicians, academics, inventors and bankers. It is an incarnation which determines our sense of structure, tradition and order, a lifetime in which our limitations and ability to concentrate were formed.

Uranus represents dominant, individualistic gods and goddesses, dramatic transformers of shape and character, eccentrics, intuitives, freedom fighters, inventive scientists, individualists, creative and independent people. It symbolizes an incarnation in which we expressed our individuality and uniqueness, and fought for freedom.

Neptune represents gods and goddesses of the psyche, of inner spiritual processes, of fantasy, imagination, romance, idealistic spirituality, mediums, mystics, dreamers and addicts. It symbolizes an incarnation in which we expressed our highest ideals and wishes, and allowed our spiritual higher self to be in control.

Pluto represents underworld gods and goddesses, transformers, revolutionaries, violent tyrants and rulers, mass murderers, warriors, statesmen and politicians. It symbolizes an incarnation in which we expressed dramatic and far-reaching changes, wanted to change the world, and carried a grand, impulsive energy for transformation.

The personal points describe our personality and ego-consciousness. The ascendant represents our personality, our personal characteristics, often our physical appearance and taste, our environmental qualities, our ways of acting and general milieu. It is an incarnation in which our self-expression was formulated, a milieu which defines the way we act and see ourselves. The mid-heaven represents our spiritual awareness, our ego-consciousness, our objectives, our sense of purpose in life and the goals of incarnation. It is an incarnation which embodies our aspirations and soul direction in life.

Let us take an example. When we have the moon in the sign Taurus (representing the period from 26,000 BC to 14,000 BC), we had a primary female incarnation at that time. During the Taurus time female-dominated earth mother cults were the primary force. The earth mother figurines from Willendorf and cave paintings at Lascaux are evidence of their existence. Agriculture was central to life and the domestication of animals was taking place. The moon is exalted in Taurus, which makes us a powerful and influential woman member of an earth mother cult. Our feelings, attitudes and response to the feminine are direct, physically powerful and dominant. We would feel that women are dominant and men inferior, and value property, possessions, sensual contacts and the tangible reality of things.

It is more difficult for a man to understand the moon in Taurus than a woman, because it involves a feminine way of feeling. A woman could integrate the qualities into her life structure quite easily, but a man with the moon in Taurus would be attracted to women who carry such qualities. The moon symbolizes our own mother as a prototype for the feminine within us.

Because Taurus is in the era of mythology, our primary incarnation would be symbolized by a moon goddess like Gaia, Ishtar, Hathor, Kali, Chthon, Io, the Moirae or Nemesis. It would be beneficial to study the myths of the lunar goddesses to understand more completely the basic feeling or energy of the moon in Taurus within us.

For planets in the era of mythology it is not so important to date the time of an incarnation exactly. There were no calendar sytems of years (a relatively recent invention) and in the mythological eras time did not really exist apart from the present moment. Humanity then had an attitude similar to that of children before the age of five today – they lived in a timeless world, immersed within reality and unable to put themselves outside of it. As history progresses towards the present time, it has speeded up, condensed and contracted to the point that we now learn to detach ourselves in objectivity as a survival device to fend off the resultant stress and existential angst. At the present time we are realizing that we must rediscover the child (or traces and behaviour patterns of the more primal beings within us), and this requires bringing history into our present and utilizing our inner historical resources in order to achieve wholeness.

NOTES

[1] Cornelius, *The Moment of Astrology*, p 178 ff.
[2] Leo, *Esoteric Astrology*, p 7.
[3] Schulman, *Karmic Astrology: Retrogrades and Reincarnation*.
[4] Ibid, p 22.
[5] See my book *Life Time Astrology* for a thorough presentation of this idea with more detail and astrological material.
[6] See my book *The Divine Plot: Astrology and Reincarnation* for a detailed description of this theory.

13 · DISCOVERING PAST LIVES

The reincarnation model described in the preceding chapter may be utilized by testing the incarnation material derived from any source, whether it be memories, regressions, dreams, fantasies, historical interest or psychotherapy. Indeed, using the astrological scale is one of the few ways to verify such experiences, apart from research into names and identities of people from the past.

Memories of incarnations from the distant past are always difficult because of the scarcity of information about individuals other than kings and queens, or heroes and heroines of mythic stature. More recent incarnations in history are easier to understand and identify, because we all have certain favourite historical times which evoke mystery and adventure to us. Those times and historical ages which have always stimulated our imaginations can be investigated first.

An example of a Renaissance odyssey emerged from my own experience. My ascendant/personality is at 6° Sagittarius. The Sagittarius time was the Renaissance, from AD 1500 to 1720, when the Age of Humanism saw great expression in art, architecture, literature and drama. Voyages of discovery opened up the world and encouraged people to rebel against traditional religions and embrace more individualistic beliefs.

From an early age I wanted to be an architect, although I did not know anyone who was. It became an obsession which informed my academic life and led to my taking an architecture degree at university. When I toured northern Italy, I felt I knew Florence and Venice and other cities intimately, almost as though I had been there before. I navigated around each as though I had lived there. Italy produced a strange feeling, like a journey into the past – the buildings were more familiar than I could express. In Rome a bizarre feeling was evoked by the Campo dei Fiori. I had friends living above this beautiful little square and it bewitched me. For some unknown reason, it was terrifying; it made me feel persecuted and in mortal danger. I spent a lot of time there, looking closely at the buildings around the piazza for some familiar sign. I noticed only a statue at the end of the piazza, but did not recognize its name.

Years later, when I became interested in astrology, I was fascinated by and read extensively about the astrologers, mystics and scientists of the 16th century, men such as John Dee, Robert Fludd, Nostradamus and Giordano Bruno. I felt I knew their minds and understood their humanist aspirations. This was especially true of Giordano Bruno, who supported Copernicus's then heretical theory that the sun was the centre of the solar system. Reading about the content of Bruno's heretical books, I felt as though I had written them myself. I then discovered that Bruno had been burnt at the stake in Campo dei Fiori in the year 1600. The statue I had seen had been erected there in his honour, centuries later.

When the reincarnation theory was first developed, I was shocked to see that my ascendant registered in 1554, during the lifetime of Bruno. Many of the architects and mystics I had been attracted to were alive at that time. It felt as though I had had a previous incarnation at that time in Italy, and the correlation of that time with my ascendant confirmed the connection. Many attitudes and beliefs, as well as my tastes in art and architecture and the need for religious freedom, traits derived from an incarnation at this time, are all primary aspects of my personality. Further investigation of this period in history have been very revealing about the qualities of this aspect of my character.

Only with the dating mechanism of the time-scale is it

possible to confirm such reincarnation experiences. While I may not necessarily have been Giordano Bruno in a previous incarnation, it felt as though I had had a past life at that time and was influenced by Bruno. It is beyond the scope of reincarnation theory to determine the actual identity of a previous incarnation, but it is clear that such aspirations correspond to those of Bruno and others alive at that time. The people with whom we relate in history signify and symbolize our previous incarnations, even if we were their servant or cousin.

THE DENSITY OF INCARNATIONS IN HISTORY

Because of the telescoping time-scale of history, a planet located in Aries-Taurus-Gemini-Cancer describes symbolic gods and goddesses which have no specific historical date. A planet in Leo-Virgo-Libra-Scorpio describes a lifetime or less in each degree of the zodiac. But a planet in Sagittarius-Capricorn-Aquarius-Pisces may describe single events rather than entire lives. If one incarnated continuously, one would probably have lived about 2,000 lives during the era of mythology, 200 during the era of civilization and 10 during the era of individuality. Since we have not incarnated this frequently, we can assume that throughout history we incarnate more and more frequently as we approach the present time. There may have been thousands of years between incarnations 40,000 years ago, but only tens of years in the last centuries.

During the last 50 years of the 20th century an unusual situation arises. During early incarnations, because of the positions of the ten planets, it would have been typical that a majority of planetary incarnations were ahead of an individual's life in time, or potential in their influence. As we approach the culmination point at the end of the 20th century, the time of a collective last judgement, all our incarnations have already been experienced. What was previously potential has been transformed into actuality. The ideal has become real. The feelings this phenomenon evoke are nostalgic, a need to return to past ideas, beliefs, styles or life patterns, or even a return to paradise, to the beginning of time before humanity became so complicated and toxic. Mircea Eliade coined the phrase 'the myth of the eternal return' to account for these feelings.

Most people are experiencing aspects of the reincarnation of all ten planets simultaneously as their previous incarnations return for the end of the world age. This may help to explain the extraordinary complexity of modern life and confirm the value of the modern psychotherapeutic concept of sub-personalities. It is also a factor in our tendency to have multiple relationships in the course of a lifetime, where in the recent past a nuclear partnership would last a lifetime. It evokes memories of our earliest history when we were nomadic and there were no clear-cut monogamous bonds.

Everyone has the ten planets, as well as the ascendant/personality and the mid-heaven/ego, so there are 12 potential incarnations determined by the astrological model. We are a blend of the various historical levels indicated by the positions of those planets, which come together and interact just as the parts of our personalities (our subpersonalities) do.

Astrological aspects are the angles between planets (eg 90 or 120) degrees which define personality patterns and describe the interrelationships of the planets in a horoscope. Some incarnation aspect connections are supportive, while others are tense and contradictory. If, for example, we have a square (tension aspect) between the sun (our father or masculine image) and the moon (our mother or feminine image), we will expect to have a inner conflict between our male and female identities. Aspects also show the relationship of our 12 incarnations to each other.

Dates determined by the reincarnation time-scale are intended to serve merely as embarkation points from which we can explore our past lives. It is beneficial to explore our past lives through techniques with which we feel comfortable, which can be hypnotic regression, reading books or meditation.

The insight required to determine our own past incarnations is beyond most people, and what is needed is a way of determining those which we can subsequently investigate. The only way to demonstrate the accuracy of the reincarnation time-scale model is to test it against some examples.

Many of the qualities which define us reflect certain historical times – they are seen in the clothes we wear, the books we read, the places to which we travel and the beliefs we choose to accept and follow. It is in determining these historical times that reincarnation theory is extremely valuable in our self-understanding.

In determining our previous incarnations, the qualities linked to such times in our karmic past may have a very wide range of manifestations. They may at first seem frivolous, but they are ultimately deep and meaningful. The qualities evoked in past lives activate an attraction we feel to those times, such as imagining ourselves as an Egyptian pharaoh or a Viking warrior, but they are ultimately carried in our being. Our romance with history may originate in our own past lives.

Our personality is the most obvious mechanism for the expression of a previous incarnation. Certain aspects of our personality derive from our family hereditary background, qualified by the environment. But we also express deeper qualities which go beyond heredity. Childhood games and adult fantasies are signals that past lives are emerging into consciousness, although most of us refuse to let the signals be expressed or stifle them from becoming more than just whims. Our past life subpersonalities may be stronger and more vital to us than we can believe. If so, it is in our interest to delve deeper into ourselves and our own history. Then we can begin to act the way we feel with assurance.

As we age, especially if we feel different or unique, we search for others who will support us, accept our individuality and resonate with our deepest feelings. The people to whom we are attracted carry parts of us, and possibly parts from our past lives – they may have been friends, lovers, parents or children. Although we are taught to ignore such feelings, they represent the expression of our true being and must be respected.

THE INCARNATIONS OF NAPOLEON

There have been many cases of famous people believing that they were incarnations of famous predecessors. Such is the case of Napoleon, who believed that he had previously incarnated as Charlemagne, and used this as a justification for declaring himself Emperor of the second Holy Roman Empire in 1804.

It must be noted that there is always a margin of error in the determination of reincarnation dates. A variation of three degrees in the location of a date represents a spread of 1 per cent on each side of a particular date. The dates derived from planetary positions can only be approximate because a lifetime occupies many degrees, and it is impossible to know when during the life of an incarnation the dated influence registers.

Napoleon believed that he had previous incarnations as Alexander the Great (356–323 BC) and Charlemagne (AD 742–812). The lifetime of Alexander the Great is from $9°$ to $10°$ of the sign Virgo, and the lifetime of Charlemagne is from $12°$ to $15°$ of the sign Libra. In Napoleon's horoscope Neptune and Mars are conjunct in Virgo – the planet Neptune occupies $8°$ of Virgo, which is translated as 377 BC. Neptune in Virgo represents psychic connections and abilities, high spiritual aspirations, dreams and fantasies, and the ability to see the future. Mars registers at $12°$ Virgo, which translates as 233 BC. Mars is the incarnation of the warrior and soldier.[1]

The ascendant (personality) in Napoleon's horoscope is at $16°$ Libra, which corresponds to AD 837. Napoleon modelled his own quest in Europe on Charlemagne's creation of the Holy Roman Empire. His personality is based on qualities derived from his previous incarnation as Charlemagne. It seems that Napoleon was justified in believing that he led past lives as Alexander and Charlemagne.

Conversely, in the horoscope of Alexander the Great there is a connection with Napoleon.[2] Alexander has Uranus at $10°$ Capricorn, equivalent to the year of Napoleon's birth! The relationship between their horoscopes demonstrates that Napoleon recognized his former life as Alexander. We could even hypothesize that Alexander could have had a premonition of his future life as Napoleon. Such reincarnation relationships exist in history and form a spiritual or psychic fabric which underlies outer events.

Past lives have a deep symbolism. They may tell us something about the kind of setting in which we choose to live or work, whether in the country, in a village or in a large metropolis. Our hobbies, our secret dreams, our taste in music, art, drama, literature or architecture all figure in the nature of our past lives. Often the job or function we performed in previous times is the reason we choose particular people, life task, art or clothes that we do.

CREATIVITY AND REINCARNATION

As creative or enquiring people we continually need to discover more about ourselves, particularly our motives for doing what we do. Reincarnation theory is a tool for directing access to the creative function in us, particularly if we call upon deeper layers of ourselves in our search for self-expression. We may find previous historical eras will activate higher levels of inspiration.

The creativity of reincarnation may be demonstrated in the horoscopes of authors, musicians, historians and other creative people. Almost by definition, authors of fiction express themselves through characters which are either autobiographical, real, imaginary, or some combination of the three. It is fascinating to see how clearly historical interests may be identified in the work of creative people. The British author, historian and poet Robert Graves (1895–1984) wrote a novel about the Roman Emperor Claudius I (10 BC–AD 54), which was dramatized for television as *I, Claudius*. Events were portrayed from the viewpoint of Claudius. Venus registers in Graves' horoscope at 16° Virgo (= 60 BC), just after the lifetime of Claudius.[3]

Many musicians have planets in the mythological era signs (Aries, Taurus, Gemini and Cancer), implying a primary means of inspiration derived by capturing early and very basic rhythms and archetypal motifs. The German composer Richard Wagner (1813–1883) was obsessed by mythological themes from early German or Teutonic legends. He has Mercury (mind and intellect) and Venus (aesthetics and music) incarnations located in the mythological sign Taurus.[4] The classic buxom Wagnerian soprano harks back to the time of the earth mothers, and the themes of many of his operas – particularly the *Ring Cycle* – evoke an early, primordial time. An opera close to his heart was *Parsifal*, about the quest of the pure knight who found the Holy Grail. Wagner based his account upon the medieval Grail legend, *Morte d'Arthur*, written in 1470. Wagner has Uranus (individuality and inspiration) located at 25° Scorpio (1460), and his ability to capture the flavour and romance of the Grail quest reflects his earlier incarnation, when he was a heretic and seeker after the truth.

The composer Giuseppe Verdi (1813–1901) captured the grandiose feeling and passion of ancient Egypt in his opera *Aida*, performances of which have included elephants and chariots drawn by horses on stage. Verdi has the planet Jupiter at 2° Virgo, which registers in 705 BC, the time when the opera action takes place.[5]

SOUL MATES AND KARMIC LINKS

In his book *Reincarnation*, Guenter Wachsmuth says:

> *Our meeting with other persons actually corresponds to a defi-*
> *nite guidance, a definite complex of laws in our inner dynamics,*
> *to be traced back to rhythms of previous existence.*[6]

Most of us long to experience profound relationships and to be able to identify our soul mate. A soul mate is someone who is so familiar, so much a part of us, that we feel we have always known him or her. Some of us are not happy unless we meet and form relationships with our soul mates.

It is important to know which qualities we share with our intimates. When we meet someone we feel strongly attracted to, we both bring karma from past lives into the relationship. In order to understand what karma is inherent in our relation-ships, it is necessary to compare our horoscope with that of our partner.

The most important karmic connections between horo-scopes are planets which are conjunct (in similar degrees of the same sign). Conjunctions are incarnations which occur at the same time in history. The planets involved show who we both were in that incarnation. If a man has Venus (his young woman) conjunct a woman's Saturn (her wise old man), in their former lives they had a relationship between the man as a young woman and the woman as a wise old man. This might explain why she may feel protective of him when they first meet. If the planets were Mars and Saturn, the relationship would have been between two men, possibly men who went to war together.

When planets are conjunct, the number of degrees they are apart determines the relative ages of the individuals in the prior incarnation. The earlier degree connotes an older person. If the degree of a planet in our horoscope is 8° and our partner's is 11° of the same sign, we can assume that in the incarnation we were older.

Rudolf Steiner and Karmic Relationships

In Rudolf Steiner's five volumes of *Karmic Relationships*, he described the action of karma in reincarnation. He believed that there are chains of karmic connections which exist from lifetime to lifetime, some convergent and others divergent. There is a rhythm in which we participate, which governs the flow towards some people and away from others. Using the reincarnation time-scale we can investigate some of his examples of linked incarnations.

Steiner developed his historical perspective through esoteric ideas. He saw the movement of ideas and spirituality as a stream flowing though history, activated by certain souls who reappear periodically and are conduits for the process of spiritual evolution. His examples correspond to harmonics of the reincarnation time-scale.

The karmic strands of knowledge linking historical movements are often separated by many centuries. Steiner identified specific times when series of individuals simultaneously discovered new ways of perceiving or explaining the world. Their inspiration was often a previous time when each significant person had an incarnation. He describes groups which incarnated together throughout history.

One such harmonic is the relationship between the mid-19th century scientists and naturalists and the Arabic philosophers of the 7th and 8th centuries AD. The mid-19th century is from $0°$ to $20°$ Aquarius, and the 7th and 8th centuries are from $10°$ to $20°$ Libra. Both are air signs and connected by trine $(120°)$ relationship, an aspect of understanding, harmony and connectedness. The trine indicates flow from one time to another. (The principle is true of connections between signs of the same element, such as water to water or fire to fire.)

Steiner identified an influential commander of the Arabs, Gebel al Tarik, after whom Gibraltar was named, and who won several battles in Spain at the beginning of the 8th century, as a predecessor of Charles Darwin. Tarik paved the way for a flourishing of culture in later centuries by expressing an attitude of the soul which subordinated brutality to art and science. According to Steiner, Tarik incarnated as Charles Darwin and brought the flowering of Arabic philosophy and natural science into the modern world. He found a flavour of the pioneer and brave warrior of this romantic time in the writings of Darwin.

Historical figures such as Tarik and Darwin complement each other. There are also karmic relationships which are in conflict in order to advance consciousness. An example of such a contact is the Caliph al Mamun (AD 790–823 or $14°$ to $16°$ Libra), the successor to the Prophet Muhammad, who cultivated astrological astronomy in his court at Baghdad. The line of the soul of Mamun leads to the modern astronomer Laplace (AD 1749–1827 or $6°$ to $25°$ Capricorn). Although Laplace's theories of astronomy were resisted, he carried the scientific spirit of the Arabs into modern times. The time of his most prolific output falls in the middle degrees of Capricorn, exactly in a square $(90°)$ relationship to the lifetime of al Mamun. The square is the relationship of tension and growth through pushing aside difficulties.

Steiner also identified the 17th century genius Francis Bacon as an incarnation of the 8th century Arabic philosopher Haroun al Raschid. Their incarnations were two signs apart, making a sextile $(60°)$ relationship, indicative of intellectual harmony and integration.

The importance of karmic relationships in modern history is advanced in *The Spear of Destiny*, written by Trevor

Ravenscroft, who was imprisoned during the Second World War in the same prisoner of war camp as Dr Johannes Stein, a teacher of Steiner's. Stein said that Hitler and the Nazi generals believed that they were incarnations of a series of historical tyrants stretching back to the time of Christ. They planned to recover the spear of the centurion Longinus, which pierced the side of Christ on the cross, and with it to conquer the world. Fortunately for us the force of destiny opposed their quest. Subsequently the book became an inspiration for Steven Spielberg's film *Raiders of the Lost Ark*.

The internal web of relationships throughout history is a fascinating study. In our horoscope, we can identify the various qualities we possess, and in history we can find the historical movements which symbolize and represent our own personal drama and mythology. The greater our understanding of our past lives and their meaning in respect of our present life, the more enlightened our next incarnation is likely to be. It is important to learn to master as many as possible of the many formative forces available to us in our long life, for the furtherance of our own ego-evolution and to serve humanity.

NOTES

[1] Napoleon, 15 August 1769, 09.50, Ajaccio, Corsica. Kampherbeek, *Cirkels*.
[2] Alexander the Great, 17 July 355 BCE, No Time, Pella, Macedonia. Rodden, *American Book of Charts*.
[3] Robert Graves, 24 July 1895, 17.00, Wimbledon, England. Rodden.
[4] Richard Wagner, 22 May 1813, 04.00, Leipzig, Germany. Rodden.
[5] Giuseppe Verdi, 10 October 1813, 20.00, Roncole, Italy. Rodden.
[6] Wachsmuth, *Reincarnation*, p 188.

14 · REINCARNATION AS METAPHOR

Reincarnation is a useful tool for enhancing our intuitive function. Once we recognize that there is a key to our historical past lives, we must follow our intuition in order to proceed. The information derived from studying reincarnation ideas is like a road map of the psyche which directs us to the area of our journey, but leaves the next choices up to us.

Reincarnation ideas can be an enriching metaphor to challenge and broaden the old horizons of what we regard as the self. The extension of consciousness into other times and the recognition of our historical reincarnation heritage can have a profound effect upon our lives. Similarly, if we avoid contact with deeper levels of our psyche, it can stunt or limit the fullness of life.

THE AMERICAN TRANSCENDENTALISTS

To illustrate how people connect through their incarnations or their common belief in reincarnation, a group of Unitarians at Harvard University founded the Transcendental Club of America in 1836. They were the authors and poets Ralph Waldo Emerson, Hedge and Ripley, and they were soon joined by Henry David Thoreau, John Greenleaf Whittier, Bronson Alcott and Walt Whitman.[1] These American Transcendentalists sought to reform the prevailing materialistic philosophy of their contemporaries by studying and expressing ideas about reincarnation from the Hindus, Greeks, Egyptians and Persians, as well as those of Kant and Goethe.

The poets Carlyle, Coleridge and Wordsworth were talked about and read as inspirational supporters of their movement in Britain. Among them they located, studied and often modified English translations of Sanskrit classics such as the *Bhagavad Gita*, the *Upanishads,* the *Vedas* and the *Puranas*. Their integration of Eastern and Western philosophy had a powerful effect upon the works of all the men involved. Emerson wrote in his journal in 1843:

> *Life itself is an interim and transition; this O Indur, is my one and twenty thousandth form, and already I feel old Life sprouting underneath in the twenty thousand and first.*[2]

It would not be too much to assume that the American Transcendentalists and their British counterparts were an incarnating soul group in the sense that Arthur Guirdham or Edgar Cayce talk about such groups. Thoreau, Carlyle, Wordsworth, Alcott and Whittier each share planets in early Sagittarius, showing a common reincarnational heritage. Emerson, Carlyle and Thoreau also share incarnations in early Gemini time, when language was first developed. Their affinity was expressed through common links with the East, and we signal our own connections to the past to others through similar ways.

When we feel an affinity with others, we should look at their lives, the art they feel close to or their horoscopes in relation to ours to discover whether we participated in such a soul group. We should also find out which periods of history we are both fascinated by because it will often indicate that we shared incarnations together.

FINDING OUR SPIRITUAL ROOTS

Our intellectual focus and artistic abilities may be derived from past lives, but our spiritual orientation, which is of even greater importance, may also be understood through reincarnation. In recent years humanity has experienced a shift in consciousness which is unparalleled in history. As the spectre of total nuclear war or global eco-disaster threatens us, humanity has experienced a spiritual explosion. People everywhere have returned to their roots, restored fundamentalist beliefs and begun believing again.

Many people have adopted ancient beliefs and committed their lives to their expansion and practice. Oriental religions have spread into the fabric of the Western world and Christianity has taken a foothold in Asian countries. It is as though every belief system created by humanity has returned and is attracting adherents. It is highly unlikely that the beliefs of our parents are the basis for our own. An opening up of the world began in about 1950, when aeroplanes began to become the primary and most efficient mode of transport. The spiritual journey to the East became a universal symbol in the 1960s and 1970s, and Jung's concept of the collective unconscious became a buzzword.

The combination of psychedelic drugs and the ease of worldwide travel made travel attractive and available to an entire generation. Many Western youths adopted the beliefs and practices of Eastern religions such as Buddhism, Taoism, Sufism and Hinduism. Many more, even in Russia, Korea, Japan and China, rediscovered Christianity, spawning the phenomenon of 'Born Again' Christians. American blacks reverted to tribal African religion, accepted Rastafarian beliefs or adopted Islamic religious practices.

The profound shift of emphsasis onto religion which has continued into the 1990s is now central to global politics. According to reincarnation theory our religious beliefs may also hold an important key to our possible past lives, allowing us to find our spiritual roots in previous incarnations.

A WESTERN TIBETAN BUDDHIST LAMA

In the 13th century, the Tibetan Buddhists first instituted spiritual techniques for selecting the successors for their lamas in their next incarnations. Upon the death of a high lama, the other lamas (occasionally in concert with the dying lama himself) determine the place and time of the birth of his successor. It can take days, months or even years for him to reincarnate, but the others use all available means to discover and locate his next incarnation, including dreams, omens and divination. The Tibetans believe that some enlightened monks can even determine exactly where and when they will be reborn and who their parents will be, in order to carry on and further their spiritual mission on earth in teaching the *dharma*. The parents may often be simple herders or nomads.

The newly incarnate lama is usually found while still an infant. He is then subjected to rigorous tests, usually involving the identification of objects belonging to the deceased from a collection of similar objects. There are many cases of the incarnate infant lamas recognizing not only these ritual and personal objects, but also the furniture, houses, friends and family of the deceased. The techniques used to determine lamaic incarnations have been kept secret over the centuries, but there is currently a dispute between the Dalai Lama and the Chinese government concerning the Dalai Lama's right to designate a young six-year-old Tibetan nomad boy as the incarnation of his former associate and spiritual master, the Panchen Lama. Paradoxically, it is the Panchen Lama who traditionally identifies the incarnations of the Dalai Lama.

A story from my own experience illustrates the principles of lamaic incarnation and also represents a powerful synchronicity. Friends of mine had a son in 1968 in Massachusetts. When he was four years old, his parents moved to Nepal and lived in Swyambhu, a Tibetan Buddhist temple complex outside of Kathmandu. Very soon after they moved there, the young boy was walking with his mother past a Tibetan Buddhist monastery. He went in and refused to leave. At his insistence, his parents enrolled him in the monastery school and he learned Tibetan ways and language extremely quickly.

The young man's mother was shocked when, in 1978, he was tracked down by Tibetan monks and identified as one of the first Westerners to be the incarnation of a high Buddhist lama. They had determined his place and time of birth correctly and had gone to Western Massachusetts to find him, only to discover that, by an apparent synchronicity, he had gone to one of their temples halfway across the world. Once identified and found, he was sent to a major monastery in Sikkim for further training in his spiritual path, so that he could disseminate Buddhist teachings throughout the world.

Many of us narrow our lives down to one particular incarnation at a specific time in history, often to the exclusion of other parts of the whole. We discover an Eastern religion, become obsessed with Chinese pottery, want to spend all our time in Mayan ruins in Mexico, or prowl around cathedrals. Through an identification with religious or cultural ideas from our hidden past reincarnations we adopt them, move back into previous ages, and signal others of a similar persuasion who are searching for a response.

All such beliefs are a primary means of identification for us, and we are often totally unaware of their higher significance. Other people with similar beliefs will support our life aims, just as we will support theirs. The immense popularity of revivalist, fundamentalist religious cults demonstrates that they allow a complete identification with a specific time in history – its beliefs, costumes, traditions and behaviour – and often allow us to immerse ourselves in the previous time and work through karmic influences which originated at that time.

The attraction of a soul to a particular religion affects the spiritual function more than any other. Such identifications exert a powerful influence and can determine the path of future incarnations. We immerse ourselves in those historical eras in which we were dominant, in control or aligned with the prevailing goals of our society rather than trying to fit in with an uninspired or spiritless modern society. It is important to identify with our own spirituality, but also to resist being immersed in particular aspects of ourselves at the expense of the whole. The soul must strive to remain aware of the eternal and avoid becoming too strongly identified with the temporal.

TAKING IN REINCARNATION

From the passing glimmer of déjà vu to profound past life regressions which open up windows to our own past, clues to our direction and glimpses of our other realities in life are always welcome. Contacts with the divine can direct us to our goals, but we have to learn how to encourage such interventions. Consciousness can isolate and confine, therefore we must sometimes invoke altered states to regain our roots in the cosmos.

Accessing the databanks of unconscious memory can enrich our mundane life and allow us to glimpse the transcendent power of visions which define history. The widening, or rather deepening, of our lives can be accomplished through recreating our internal history.

There are books which can direct us to experiential paths of reincarnation, such as *Your Past Lives*, by Michael Talbot, *The Case for Reincarnation* by Joe Fisher, or *Magick* by Aleister Crowley. But once we begin to experience reincarnation phenomena it is essential that we evaluate our resultant perceptions and integrate them sensibly into the whole of our psyche.

Past life therapists use a variety of techniques to induce memories of previous incarnations, including hypnosis, meditation, rebirthing, reflexology, massage or psychotherapy. We may find that it is easier than we expect, and deep meditation may provoke experiences that will change our lives. Once a past-life experience is evoked, it is important to deepen our understanding of it through further study and exercises. While individual incarnative experiences are valuable and can be enlightening, it would seem to be more beneficial to gain an overview of our lives in history so that the path of our souls may be divined and travelled again.

NOTES

[1] Head and Cranston, *Reincarnation: The Phoenix Fire Mystery*, pp 309–21.
[2] Ibid, p 311.

BIBLIOGRAPHY

RELIGION, PHILOSOPHY AND MYTH

Ballou, Robert O (Ed), *The Bible of the World*, Kegan Paul Trench Trubner, London, 1940

Campbell, Joseph, *The Mythic Image*, Princeton, Princeton, 1974

Eliade, Mircea, *From Primitives to Zen*, Collins, London, 1967

— *The Sacred and the Profane*, trans Willard Trask, Harcourt Brace & World, 1959

Evans-Wentz, W Y (Ed), *The Tibetan Book of the Dead*, Commentary by C G Jung, Oxford University Press, London, 1960

Fabricius, Johannes, *Alchemy*, Rosenkilde & Bagger, Copenhagen, 1976

Fodor, Nandor, *Freud, Jung and Occultism*, University Books, New York, 1971

Frazer, James G, *The Golden Bough: A Study of Magic and Religion*, Macmillan, London, 1950

Hick, John, *Death and Eternal Life*, Collins, London, 1976

Hoeller, Stephan A, *The Gnostic Jung and the Seven Sermons to the Dead*, Theosophical Publishing, Wheaton, 1972

Jocelyn, Beredene, *Citizens of the Cosmos*, Continuum, New York, 1981

Jordan, Michael, *Myths of the World*, Kyle Cathie, London, 1993

Jung, C G, *Alchemical Studies*, trans R F C Hull, Routledge & Kegan Paul, London, 1973

—, *Psychology and Alchemy*, CW 13, trans R F C Hull, Routledge & Kegan Paul, London, 1974

—, *Seven Sermons to the Dead*, Stuart & Watkins, London, 1973

Jung, Emma and von Franz, Marie Louise, *The Grail Legend*, trans Andrea Dykes, G P Puttnams, New York, 1970

Mann, A T and Lyle, Jane *Sacred Sexuality*, Element, Shaftesbury, 1995

Mead, G R S, *Orpheus*, John M Watkins, London, 1965

Pagels, Elaine, *The Gnostic Gospels*, Penguin, London, 1979

Robinson, James M, (Director), *The Nag Hammadi Library in English*, E J Brill, Leiden, 1977

Róheim, Géza, *Animism, Magic and the Divine King*, Routledge & Kegan Paul, London, 1930

Schwaller de Lubicz, Isha, *The Opening of the Way*, trans Rupert Gleadow, Inner Traditions, New York, 1979

Schwaller de Lubicz, R A, *Sacred Science*, trans André and Goldian VandenBroeck, Inner Traditions, New York, 1982

—, *Symbol and Symbolic*, trans Robert Lawlor, Autumn Press, Brookline, 1978

—, *The Temple in Man*, trans Robert and Deborah Lawlor, Autumn Press, Brookline, 1977

Sogyal Rinpoche, *The Tibetan Book of Living and Dying*, HarperCollins, San Francisco, 1993

Walker, Barbara G, *The Woman's Encyclopedia of Myths and Secrets*, Harper & Row, San Francisco, 1983

Warner, Rex, (Ed), *Encyclopaedia of World Mythology*, BPC Publishing, London, l975

West, John Anthony, *Serpent in the Sky*, Harper & Row, New York, 1979

—, *The Travelers's Key to Ancient Egypt*, Alfred A Knopf, New York, 1985

Zimmer, Heinrich, *Myths and Symbols in Indian Art and Civilization*, ed Joseph Campbell, Bollingen, Washington, 1946

—, *Philosophies of India*, ed Joseph Campbell, Meridian Books, New York, 1956.

ASTROLOGY, MAGIC AND METAPHYSICS

Bauval, Robert and Gilbert, Adrian, *The Orion Mystery*, William Heinemann, London, 1994

Collin, Rodney, *The Theory of Celestial Influence*, Stuart & Watkins, London, 1968

ASTROLOGY

Cornelius, Geoffrey, *The Moment of Astrology*, Arkana, London, 1995

Crowley, Aleister, *Magick*, Samuel Weiser, York Beach, 1986

Kampherbeek, Jan, *Cirkels*, Uitgeverij Schors, Amsterdam, 1980
Leo, Alan, *Esoteric Astrology*, Astrologers Library, New York, 1913
LeShan, Lawrence, *Alternate Realities*, Ballantine, New York, 1976
Mann, A T, *Life Time Astrology*, Element, Shaftesbury, 1991
Rodden, Lois, *The American Book of Charts*, ACS, San Diego, 1980
Schulman, Martin, *Karmic Astrology: Retrogrades and Reincarnation*, Samuel Weiser, New York, 1977

REINCARNATION

Collin, Rodney, *The Theory of Eternal Life*, Watkins, London, 1974
Currie, Ian, *You Cannot Die*, Element, Shaftesbury, 1994
Fisher, Joe, *The Case for Reincarnation*, Introduction by Dalai Lama, Bantam, New York, 1984
Langley, Noel, *Edgar Cayce on Reincarnation*, Warner, New York, 1967
Mann, A T, *The Divine Plot: Astrology and Reincarnation*, Element Shaftesbury, 1991
Ravenscroft, Trevor, *The Spear of Destiny*, Neville Spearman, London, 1968
Steiner, Rudolf, *Earthly and Cosmic Man*, trans. Dorothy Osmond, Rudolf Steiner Publishing, London, 1948
...*Karmic Relationships*, trans. George Adams, Anthroposophical Publishing, London, 1955
...*The Spiritual Hierarchies and Their Reflection in the Physical World: Zodiac, Planets, Cosmos*, Anthroposophic Press, NY, 1970
Talbot, Michael, *Your Past Lives*, Ballantine Books, New York, 1987
Wachsmuth, Guenther, *Reincarnation*, trans. Olin Wannamaker, Philosophic-Anthroposophic Press, Dornach, 1937
Wambach, Helena, *Reliving Past Lives: The Evidence Under Hypnosis*, Harper & Row, New York, 1978

INDEX

135